THE 80/20 INVESTOR

Investing in an uncertain and complex world — *How to simplify investing with a single principle.*

By: David Schneider

TESTIMONIALS

"Just as the internet has democratized work, it has also democratized investing. We are raised to believing that investing intelligently is complex and difficult, something best left to professionals. In the 80/20 investor, David shows that for those who take the 80/20 approach, investing is now easier, more fun and more profitable than ever." —**Taylor Pearson, author of The End of Jobs**

"When it comes to financial planning, freelancers and entrepreneurs are particularly vulnerable. In his pleasant and patient writing style, David Schneider lays out a no-stress investment plan that anyone can follow. Invest in your future – get this book." —**André Gussekloo, co-author of Digital Nomads: How to Live, Work and Play Around the World**

Investments can be confusing and risky business. Right from Chapter 1 David lays down easy to understand, highly actionable advice, tactics and strategies that cut through the noise and help simplify otherwise complex and confusing investment decisions. **Brendan Tully, Principal Consultant —The Search Engine Shop**

David breaks down what some people spend their lifetime into succinct chapters of how to cut out the B.S. of investing. Most of us are busy with our professions and building our careers but want to tap into the financial markets - I'm confident that after they read this book they'll be well equipped to be ahead of the pack! —**Mike Michelini host at Global From Asia**

The 80/20 Investor helps entrepreneurs to become better investors in their own enterprises. Japanese investors and entrepreneurs will surely find this book valuable. —**Tatsuro Tsushima, Managing Director of INDEE Japan and co-supervisor of The First Mile**

" The 80/20 investor is going to be a valuable food for thought for any kind of business or individual, regardless of age or volume of wealth. David has done a remarkable job delivering the 80/20 principle in such a way that practically anyone can put it into use and make great things happen." —**Angelos GkOne, Software Entrepreneur and creator of X-Bricks**

"Mark Twain once said: "Whenever you find yourself on the side of the majority, it is time to pause and reflect." That's exactly what this book does. It challenges the common way of thinking about investing.

I used to feel the pressure to always have my money invested. I don't feel that anymore. The 80/20 approach radically changed my view on investing. It gave me the necessary peace of mind, clarity, and knowledge to wait the right moment to invest. Now I know when to do it, and how to do it." —**Marco Zamboni, Web Entrepreneur**

"David Schneider offers a satisfying contemporary approach to investing. You'll be fiercely conditioned to make the smartest choices with your money." —**Lee Constantine, Publishizer, Inc**

CONTENTS

INTRODUCTION

A pig farmer's approach to investing

"Mr. Hogan, would you like to see a man who has never lost money in the stock market?"

Mr. Hogan looked up, baffled. Who was that? The voice was coming from across the way. Some senior account manager at Merrill Lynch. But that guy had never spoken to him before.

Too bad, thought Hogan, he could have done with some advice. He'd done well enough since the end of World War II. Discharged from the army, he'd gone into oil rig construction and dabbled in stocks. His friends, coworkers, and even business partners seemed to be boasting of easy capital gains and they convinced him to join in the stock market game. To his dismay, he seemed to lose money every time he followed the advice of others. He tried to copy his friends, while following the advice of his broker and star fund managers at that time, but at the end of each year he always had a net loss. He tried every approach he read or heard about: technical, fundamental, and combinations of all these, but he always managed to end up with a loss. Even in the great rally of 1958, with the Dow Jones performing better than 25%, he somehow pulled a net loss.

Yeah, he would like to meet someone who'd never lost on the stock market. But who the hell was this guy?

'Would you like to see that man?' the voice repeated.

'Never had a loss?' stammered Hogan.

But what he was really thinking was - Yes, please! And tell me his secrets, too.

"Never had a loss on balance, and I have handled his account for nearly 40 years." The broker gestured to a hulking man dressed in overalls, who was sitting among the crowd of tape watchers.

"If you want to meet him, you'd better hurry," he advised. "He rarely visits our office when he's not buying or selling. He only hangs around a few minutes to check out the tape and some company information. So you better hurry up before you miss him. He's a rice farmer and hog raiser from down around Baytown."

A curious, but wary Mr. Hogan worked his way through the crowd to find a seat beside the stranger in overalls. He nervously fiddled with his portfolio sheet until he finally mustered the courage to talk to the farmer.

To his surprise, the stranger, Mr. Womack, was happy to talk about stocks. Mr. Womack pulled a sheet of paper from his pocket with a pencil-scrawled list of stocks that he had just finished selling and let Mr. Hogan look at it.

He couldn't believe his eyes. The man had made over 50 long-term capital gain profits on the whole group! One stock in the group of 30 stocks disappointed and showed up as a loss, but others had gone up to 100%, 200%, and even up to 500%.

Mr. Womack explained his technique, which was pure simplicity. During a bear market, he would read in the papers that the market was down to new lows, and the experts were predicting that it was sure to drop another 200 points in the Dow, then the farmer would look through the Standard & Poor's Stock Guide and select around 30 stocks that had fallen in price substantially. He would choose those that were profit-making and would pay regular dividends. He would then come to Houston and buy a $25,000 "package" of them.

And then, two, three, or four years later, when the stock market was bubbling and the prophets were talking about the Dow hitting new records, he would come to town to his broker and sell his whole package.
It was as simple as that.

Mr. Hogan remained friends with Mr. Womack until his death. During that time, he learnt a lot from Mr. Womack, who always had a great analogy from his farming work that applied to his stock investing strategy. One day while hunting ducks, Mr. Womack had another analogy ready. This time, it was his hog raising business for which he was renowned for his skills and experience among his farming community. He equated buying stocks with buying a truckload of pigs. The lower he could buy the pigs, when the pork market was depressed, the more profit he would make when the next seller's market would come along. He claimed that he would rather buy stocks under these conditions, because pigs did not pay a dividend. Plus, you have to feed pigs.

Mr. Womack took "a farming approach" to investing. In rice farming, there is a planting season and a harvesting season. Mr. Womack, in his purchases and sales, strictly observed the seasons.

He never achieved the best possible bottom prices and he was never able to sell his investments at top prices, either. He didn't aim to! Mr. Womack seemed happy to buy or sell at good average prices. When prices continued to drop, he simply ignored the old stock market cliché "Never send good money after bad" and continued buying into falling prices. He was happy to have found a productive home for his cash savings.

When the market continued to decline substantially in the 1970s, for example, Mr. Womack added another $25,000 out of his cash savings to his previous bargain-priced positions, and made a fortune on the whole package when the market rose again. Even if it took several years to materialize, he was comfortable holding stocks instead of keeping his savings in cash.

Mr. Womack didn't make investing work-intensive or complicated for himself. He didn't have a finance or MBA degree, nor did he rely on brokers or bankers for his investment decisions. He intuitively understood that the stock market was a place, like a farmers market, to occasionally take advantage of. He understood that only very few actions determine investment success, and to focus on these and to ignore anything else. That way, he could spend his time on what he did best and was trained to do -- which was raising pigs and farming.

Among the most important things Mr Womack taught Mr. Hogan was that, "you couldn't buy assets every day, week, or month of the year and make a profit, any more than you could plant rice every day, week, or month and make a crop."

If you asked a hundred professional money managers today what the single best investment strategy is, and what would be the core component of that strategy's success, I suppose you would hear many different answers. On top of that, some of their explanations would be so complex, it would make a finance professor proud.

But nobody I know in the professional money management field would put emphasis on the simple "**buy price,**" according to specific seasons that Mr. Womack practiced.

He was what I'd call an 80/20 Investor. Someone who focused only on the few tasks that made the biggest impact on his performance. It simplified everything for him and made him a wealthy pig farmer.

This book is about 80/20 Investors, their simple approach, and how you can become one, too. (Sorry, it's not about pigs and farming!) [1]

PART I:
A SIMPLE PERSPECTIVE ON INVESTING

CHAPTER 1:
Why you should read this book

"The individual has always had to struggle to keep from being overwhelmed by the tribe. If you try it, you will be lonely often, and sometimes frightened. But no price is too high to pay for the privilege of owning yourself."

—FRIEDRICH NIETZSCHE

"How should I invest my cash in these market conditions?"

This is a common question that individual investors often ask themselves. With all the warnings of possible inflation eating up their hard-earned cash, and having friends, professionals, and financial media recommend they take action sooner rather than later, who can blame them?

When I hear this question, I always reply by asking what they have been doing to attain the current amount. Whatever their answer is, I tell them to continue doing what they have done so far.

The simple reason is that their techniques must be working for them; otherwise, they wouldn't have accumulated the cash in the first place. This is not the standard answer they're hoping for, or even expecting, from an investment professional.

But how many a fortune has been created by simply focusing on what people have been able to do best.

By working their day jobs or building businesses, reinvesting in themselves or in their own companies, and saving a large chunk of their income, countless people like this have achieved financial freedom without following the calls of their financial and investment advisors to do anything differently.

It is more prudent to focus on the primary cash income, which is generated by you or your own business (what I call a "cash engine" in later chapters), than to divert your attention away to areas that are beyond your training and expertise. This could potentially harm your long-term wealth.

Unfortunately, the low interest environment we live in today has made it painfully clear that a basic education in investing is vital to secure our personal financial freedom, and to help future generations attain similar goals. Over the last 10 years or so, masses of individual savers have entered a field of investing barely prepared, technically or psychologically, for a field that is famous for not taking any prisoners.

According to a survey I did among my readers in October 2015, I found out that 30% would be able to spend less than 10 hours week on their investment management work, while 61% would be able to spend less than two hours a week on their investment strategy. This is not much compared to professional investment advisors and investment bankers, who work regular 60-hour weeks or more and have superior resources to do their job.

On top of that, my survey revealed that 23% of the readers who responded have return expectations of 5% or higher, and 58% have return expectations of 10% or more. In comparison, leading US stock indices, such as the famous S&P500 or the Dow Jones Industrial Average, which is comprised of the 30 leading publicly listed companies of the US, yielded less than 8% over the last 20 years, but less than 6% annualized returns over the last 10 years swamped with liquidity by Central Banks never seen before. And don't forget that over 70% of professional managers are not able to beat this performance history, especially after all the fees they charge.

It is clear that there is a mismatch between work input and return expectations.

To overcome this mismatch, consumers do what they usually do, if they are faced with a complex and time consuming challenge. They ask a professional!

The lack of independent thinking and decision making is frightening. The masses of existing individual investors seem to be wandering around in a feverish haze, induced by a fixation on celebrity investors. All the while, these celebrity investors promote investment strategies designed to benefit their own portfolios.

Since the subprime crises, every consumer should be aware of how the financial industry ticks and how their incentives are structured. However, individual investors, and even established entrepreneurs, rely too much on advice or completely pass all responsibility for their investment portfolios to so-called professionals. Unfortunately, on average they generate appalling results with layers of fees that could be higher than 3% before a single investment is done for their clients. The reality is that finding truly talented and capable managers is as difficult as finding the right investments they are themselves searching for.

To make matters worse, the current challenging market environment causes head scratching among retail investors and professionals alike, even though they would never admit it. The movements of asset prices going up and down, to the dollar's strength or weakness, interest rate changes, declining commodity prices, or China's economy cooling down, are all on investors minds. Add to this the constant warnings of financial Armageddon, or the promotion of the next possible Facebook or Google type investment opportunities by some self-declared investment gurus depicted on TV, and the confusion is complete. We most certainly live in an uncertain and contradictory world.

In this chaos, a growing number of individual investors have made it their mission to mirror the strategies of successful investment personalities celebrated in financial news and media. Yet, should the average individual investor be copying the techniques of professional Value, Growth, or Quantitative investors? Should we be copying the erratic outbursts of a Jim Cramer, who seems to jump from one stock to another with each TV performance? Or do we have the cold blooded investment wit of a Kevin O'Leary? Do we understand how the economy works in meticulous detail as Billionaire Hedge Fund Manager Ray Dalio? Do we have the billions to invest, and the mental capacity, of a Warren Buffett? Most likely not.

Ask yourself if this is what an average individual investors should and can do. The clear answer is no!

The average person has neither the time, the background, nor the resources to fully mirror those strategies. We all have our own normal jobs and lives.

Now you likely ask yourself, is there an investment approach that is easy to understand, that even a busy entrepreneur or employed individual could practice without the need for professional help and specialized training, and which doesn't make their life miserable? An approach that can help us navigate a minefield of traps, scams, overpriced assets, and incompetent investment advice?

The short answer is yes.

What would you think if I told you that you could get similar returns as professionals, at a fraction of the cost? Not only that, but also at a fraction of the time and effort spent?

It's called 80/20 Investing.

Since I started working in the investment industry more than 15 years ago, I have been experimenting with and testing the most common trading and investment strategies ranging from chart analysis, options trading, value to momentum, and risk arbitrage.

I scratched my head about the sheer complexity and chance involved in some of the more complex investment strategies. I admit, I wasn't very successful with these time and labor intensive strategies and I am not the most assiduous person by nature, especially when I feel it's work I shouldn't have to do!

Whether small or large, I always try to accomplish my goals in the least work-intensive way. I have brought this attitude to my investment work with some astounding results and insights.

The missing principle

Through my own work experience, I have come to realize that time-tested, simple investment principles still work today. They require a minimum of work and are surprisingly easy to apply.

In 2010, while reading *The 4-Hour Workweek* by Timothy Ferriss, I reacquainted myself with a forgotten principle. It was a principle I was familiar with from my days at university, but I didn't fully comprehend its application at that time. Pareto's Principle, also known as the 80/20 principle, demonstrates that only a minority of causes lead to the majority of results. Everywhere in life.

I have come to realize that 20%, or actually much less work, to manage an investment portfolio will generate more than 80% of the performance. Only a few factors contribute to extraordinary investment success.

My theory was confirmed when I analyzed all my own historic investments over the last 15 years. I realized that the few, highly successful performance generating investments were all in accordance with the 80/20 principle to investing. I am not talking about those countless little trades here and there we all like to do as investors. Yes, they made me some money, most of the time through sheer luck. They satisfied my lust for gambling and speculation, but frankly they had no sizeable impact on the entire performance. No, I am referring to the large investments, with a huge impact on the entire investment portfolio.

Introducing Vilfredo Pareto's Principle to investing

Indeed, Vilfredo Pareto's Principle, also known as 80/20 rule, explains the fundamental concept of money and investing.

There are countless observations in all aspects of our lives. For example, in sales, 20% of salespeople seem to make more than 80% of all sales commission. Also, in global wealth distribution, less than 10% of the world's population controls more than 90% of the world's assets, varying from country to country. Even in our daily work lives, 20% of all actions we do contribute to 80% of our daily results.

Richard Koch, the author of *Living the 80/20 Way, Work Less, Worry Less, Succeed More, Enjoy More*, made similar observations in his book, and had a simple proposition in regards to handling our money.

He said, "Because of compound interest, money becomes concentrated in few hands. There is therefore one, and only one, infallible 80/20 route to enough money — to save and invest in the easiest possible way." [2]

Investing in this way has the potential to free any person from stress, work, over-complicated theories, and reliance on brokers, consultants, or other soothsayers, while still seeing competitive annualized returns.

Unfortunately, even though Koch gave some specific examples on how to save money the 80/20 way, and explained the power of compound interest, he didn't give specifics on how to invest in the easiest way possible. And, more importantly, on how to invest the 80/20 way.

This book builds upon Koch's thoughts, providing an approach to investing the 80/20 way where we identify our 80/20 goal, the easiest way to get there and specific tasks to be executed.

Book Outline

In this book, I will start by discussing two simple assumptions.

1) Saving and investing is the key to financial freedom -- it is the 80/20 way!

2) Saving and investing itself is simple if we apply the 80/20 principle.

I will discuss the need for and advantages of a rudimentary investment education, and why we need to make decisions independently of professional advisors.

Following these discussions, the book is divided into three sections, which outline a 3-step process to becoming an 80/20 Investor.

Step 1. Set your investment destination
Step 2. Identify the steps necessary to reach that destination
Step 3. Take action

By studying past and present 80/20 Investors and by comparing them with professional investment managers today, we will be able to set our destination.

Once our destination is set, we will identify the tasks necessary to reach our goals.

The final step is to execute the action points set down from step 2. In the section on this step, I will give advice and tips to individual investors on how they can take action the easiest way possible.

I will discuss the topic of investors psychology and its influence on our decision making. I will also recommend techniques on how to better control and reduce the interference of emotions when making buying or selling decisions.

Finally, I will explain why the 80/20 principle of investing really works, and why it is possible to get competitive returns with a fraction of the work done by professionals.

This book is aimed at individuals who have very little time to handle their own private investment operation, but don't want to rely on professional help or pay for expensive academic courses. It is specifically aimed at individual investors and entrepreneurs who have day jobs and businesses to take care of, and don't want to spend hours in front of their computer screens chasing hot investment ideas. It is also for all individuals who are willing to break with the norms of today's investor culture.

I will demonstrate that the 80/20 approach requires no special infrastructure, running expenses, or expensive advice. Most importantly, it is an approach that doesn't require you to constantly anticipate and forecast what under complex assumptions the world economy, your industry, or specific investment will do next. This is an approach even a laidback backpacker currently hiking somewhere in the Andes could apply without spending sleepless nights thinking about his or her investments.

It is explained in understandable language, without much jargon, and with lots of case studies, investment anecdotes, and references for further reading. All that is required from the reader is common sense, some discipline, and self-awareness.

CHAPTER 2:
The 80/20 Way

Having more money doesn't necessarily make you happier, but more time can!

—UNKNOWN

We all know the expression -- time is money, and money is time. In modern society, we have adopted a lifestyle where we seemingly sacrifice our time to make more money, believing that more money and more consumption will make us happier. Excuses range from driving the latest car, having a great apartment, going on exotic vacations, or just giving your children the most expensive education possible -- the list is endless.

This high standard of living and emphasis on overconsumption in developed countries comes at a price, and is more often than not financed with debt.

This usually results in a vicious cycle of more spending, more debt, and more work. Short-term gratification is all the rage. However, long lasting happiness looks different.

Debt is also the main reason why so many of us in western societies still endure the omnipresent "rat race," defined as an endless, self-defeating, and usually pointless pursuit of money.

Conventional thinking dictates that there must always be a compromise between reaping the fruits of society and paying the price, and most of us have come to accept it as an unshakable fact. Sadly, this conventional way of thinking is based on two main misconceptions.

First, we have become slaves to the dictum: "more makes us happier."

Second, in order to achieve more, we believe that there is a linear relationship between work input and output.

Nothing could be further from the truth. Koch in his book *Living the 80/20 Way*, clears up these misconceptions.

He claims that living the 80/20 way "breaks the logjam" [4] and that it offers more life energy for less effort. Specifically on the topic of money, he demands that, "instead of money ruling our lives by making work stressful or miserable, we should use money to regain control of life." He adds, "However much or little we earn, we can save, invest, and multiply money. Through saving and investing money, we avoid trading our life energy for money."

What he was referring to was gaining financial freedom through harnessing the power of the 80/20 principle. It doesn't mean that you have so much money coming in you don't have to work anymore. It means having the freedom to do what you really want in life, and the freedom to be the person you are striving to be.

What Koch postulates is that, regardless of age or whatever lifestyle you are aiming for, the solution to your individually-defined financial freedom can be achieved by saving and investing money. It represents the best and the most effective way.

First, let's understand the 80/20 principle definition, what Koch calls "one of the most mind-blowing, far reaching, and surprising discoveries of the past 200 years."

Indeed, the 80/20 principle can be found in all facets of life. If you know what you are trying to achieve, you can focus your attention on the 20% that brings most of the results.

Don't worry if the numbers do not perfectly match the 80/20 ratio. According to Perry Marshall, the author of *80/20 Sales and Marketing*, "[i]t's not the exact number 80/20 that's the rule; it's the principle of positive feedback, which is when behavior is rewarded so that it produces more of the same behavior. Sometimes it's 60/40 or

70/30; sometimes it's 90/10 or 95/5. The exact numbers aren't so important. But it's always there." [5]

The only thing you have to do is identify these tasks. We have to ask ourselves one single question, according to Koch: "What will give us better result for less energy?" or, in a more common phrase: "How do we get the most bang for our buck?"

If the 80/20 principle says that 80% of your results come from 20% of your efforts, what if we continued to play this game and isolated 20% of the first 20%? According to Marshall, the 80/20 principle still applies to a higher degree. "The real power in 80/20 is that you can disregard 80% of the roads in your city; only look at the top 20%, and the 80/20 rule will still apply. 80% of the 80% of traffic is on 20% of the 20% of roads. That means 64% of the travelers drive on 4% of the roads. That's 80/20 squared." (We should keep this in mind when we look at compound tables and the final task list, which can be found in the appendix.)

In recent years, the 80/20 principle has gained popularity in business, economics, and among digital nomads and location independent entrepreneurs. It has even seen a rise in popularity in self-help books for improving relationships and general happiness. But does it work for money and investing?

The 80/20 principle itself was born out of the observation of how land, a classic fixed asset, was distributed. Vilfredo Pareto's original study in 1906 found that 80% of the land in Italy was owned by 20% of the population. Land is considered a classic investment asset among the wealthy and powerful.

He also found out that 20% of people enjoyed 80% of the money. The 80/20 principle is a determining factor for the distribution of money that will give us some clues on how to understand the principles of money and how we can utilize it in our own investment approach.

Need for investing education

In a simple definition, investing is often described as the process of laying out money for assets now, in the expectation of receiving more money in the future. In a perfect world, the process of investing, besides its financial incentives, allows for the efficient distribution of access capital to where it is needed most and to where it supports the progress of human civilization in the form of innovation and the exchange of ideas. Investing is a vital act, important for world organizations, single states, communities, and individuals.

To me, income from investing is the ultimate path to wealth and financial freedom for anybody who aspires a location independent lifestyle or an improved work-life balance. You can climb Mt. Kilimanjaro and not have to worry about your investments; you know your money is working for you. You can set up a new business venture in Hong Kong and you don't have to constantly check back on what your invested capital is doing. You can spend time with your family, on your latest health project, or just focus on the things that matter most to you. The investment returns are flowing to your pockets with or without your constant attention.

Just imagine that along the way, through persistent saving and investing, your additional income from investing is approaching a level that matches your current monthly expenditure. It would open up a totally new perspective on your existing job and what you consider to be your priorities in life.

In order to reap investing's benefits, it is necessary to seriously apply oneself to learning about the basics of investment management and its impact on our lives. Most governments in western countries are basically bankrupt. They won't be able to guarantee you a safe retirement like your parents might be enjoying right now. This makes a rudimentary education in savings and investing necessary for all future generations.

However, can we rely on Wall Street to educate us, to take care of our money and our retirement concerns? Can we take advice at face value from an industry which is responsible for most of the economic disasters in the last two centuries? Unfortunately not. Now, it's easy to bash and pass the blame on to an entire industry that sells us financial products we don't need and often causes losses. But, in the end, it is our own responsibility, our own decisions.

Whether you are from Generation Y or the generations before it, you need to take charge of your own money affairs. Whether you want to manage your excess cash, are concerned about your retirement, or aim for financial freedom, it is mandatory to educate yourself and develop skills for investing.

Every private person should be educated in cash management and investing to develop an additional source of income that will help achieve financial freedom in the easiest and the most efficient way. More importantly, we need to be independent of whoever wants to manipulate us or tries to take advantage of our financial concerns and limited investment education by trying to sell us products and services we don't need. A basic education in investing will help you distinguish the "BS advice" and tips from quality information and services.

Investing for Entrepreneurs

For business owners and entrepreneurs, applying the 80/20 principle to saving and investing has additional advantages.

All successful entrepreneurs know that at some stage in the business cycle, instead of lacking cash, they will be overwhelmed by it. It may seem to be a luxurious problem to have, but it is a serious one nevertheless.
The question will then arise: what to do with all the excess cash? Redeploy it into one's own business? Start a new business or maybe even buy another business in the same industry in a different country? Or enter something entirely unrelated?

From overexpansion at the wrong time, to idiotic deals that shouldn't have been made in the first place, at no other stage in a business cycle have there been more serious mistakes made than when investing one's surplus cash. All successful business owners and operations managers seem to know how to create businesses and manage complex operations, but many lack the skills to successfully invest their surplus capital.

From an economic, as well as a lifestyle point of view, correctly deploying more cash in one's own business is harder than it sounds.

There are a large number of small to midsize businesses that generate impressive excess cash, most of them family owned businesses. However, these businesses are ill equipped for expansion. Expanding with brute force (i.e., to continue investing where there is no demand and the prospect of shrinking markets) is equal to committing economic suicide. In such situations, a specific business niche has been filled, or the market has matured and is oversaturated. There is simply no growth potential to go ahead without hurting business returns. In worst case scenarios it could lead to killing the "golden goose" by taking on additional risks due to aggressive overexpansion.

The solution is to invest the company's cash effectively. In business circles, this is referred to as "capital allocation" -- deploying funds where it can generate the best returns at minimum risk. That could be within one single industry, cross industries, or even regions.

Learning how to properly and effectively allocate capital will make us more successful. We will be more aware of our own management styles and we will be more aware of all financial aspects related to the management of profitable businesses.

Conclusion

We have seen that the 80/20 principle exists all around us and that it plays a vital role in money and money management. Understanding that an elementary education in investing is necessary and beneficial for both individuals and entrepreneurs, we will now find out how the 80/20 principle really works in investing, and how we can harness its power.

CHAPTER 3:
How to apply the 80/20 principle to investing

A journey of a thousand miles begins with a single step.

—LAOZI

If the 80/20 way to financial freedom is a way of saving and investing, can we then apply the 80/20 principle on these two separate components as well? Are we able to develop a savings and investment approach that is built around the 80/20 principle?

In the universe of possible tasks that you could perform in investing, which tasks contribute to performance the most? Is it the financial modelling work using Excel spreadsheets, or forecasting every accounting detail 10 years in advance with various assumptions? Or is it the technical analysis that some investors use? If you made a list of the possible work tasks that go into detailed analysis, including those performed by professionals, you would realize that there are hundreds.

However, common sense, and the awareness that the 80/20 principle exists all around us, would suggest that only a few tasks contribute to investment performance the most.

Have you ever wondered why some of us are extremely rich by only doing one thing right? Have you ever wondered how a person, with a single investment decision, can go from rags to riches? They are not only the "Masters of the Universe" as the media presents them to us, but also common folks. Countless entrepreneurs and family businesses made fortunes with one single investment decision. Their decision was to invest in their own business and to keep improving their cash flow potential.

Think about the very early investors in Berkshire Hathaway; some were housewives, some lawyers or mechanics, and they all made a single investment decision when they invested in Warren Buffett's partnerships, and later in Berkshire Hathaway. Those early investors are now rich beyond their wildest imaginations, and they have gotten there with only a single decision.

Those who sold their shares early because they were worried about a financial crisis that occurred over the course of Berkshire's 50 years, or simply followed an active buying and selling approach, have since regretted their selling decision.

Apple never revisited - The story of Mr. Standingback

Consider the story of an acquaintance of mine, who bought Apple Inc. shares in late 1998, long before the first iPod was launched.

Let's call him Mr. Standingback. As a freelance editor and proofreader based in the UK, he was an early admirer of Apple's Macs, their stylish interface and fonts, their user friendly Operating System (OS), and their new and colorful designs. He genuinely liked the company, its products, and its eccentric CEO, Steve Jobs.

He decided to purchase Apple shares for an amount of $10,000, financed by his cash savings. He felt comfortable with his Apple investment without fearing for his future retirement, because he had always been a good saver. Furthermore, he felt that he got his shares for a good price, and he was sure that Apple had a bright future.

Yet, he decided to sell all his shares just a year later, when they doubled in value. He couldn't resist to cash in his book profits. That was in late 1999, before the Dotcom bubble peaked. He thought he made a big profit and should be investing somewhere else in this market environment. He lost most of his newly invested funds in the following months, when the bubble finally burst at the end of 2000.

With hindsight, you would ask yourself why he was so impatient and sold his shares for such a pittance. Well, if you saw your own stocks today with a fat 100% plus in your portfolio, you might equally be tempted to sell. But I ask you, would you sell your own business, just someone told you it has doubled in value, even though you knew it is worth much more. You didn't see Steve Jobs running to his brokers to sell his personal Apple shares.

In the aftermath of the dotcom bubble, Apple fell back from a peak of about $9.90 a share to $1.20 by early 2001. Mr. Standingback read about the iPod launch the same year, and he knew that it was a winner, but he couldn't bring himself to get back into investing after his painful experiences. When the markets recovered and news reported of a fantastic market turnarounds and great stock market gains, he finally started investing again. This time with more vigor and enthusiasm than ever before just to play catch up. He invested in everything, especially in companies he didn't understand, except for Apple shares, which would have been the most logical choice. Somehow, there was a mental block that didn't allow him to just repurchase his Apple shares at a higher price than what he originally paid for.

Things went well for a couple of years, but, unfortunately, he reacted in a similar way in 2008: panic. In the wake of the financial crisis of 2008, he panicked and sold his stocks, most of them with substantial losses. At the same time, Apple dropped from its new peak of over $27 a share in 2007 to $12 a share during early 2009 (*prices adjusted for splits).

Last year, I heard that Mr. Standingback got back into investing in stocks big time, when the stock market had finally recovered from the aftermath of the subprime crises. Placing the setbacks of 2009 behind him, he started investing again in in the middle of 2013. He seems to be enthused by the book gains he has made so far, and he is eager to invest more of his monthly savings. He is already calculating himself into retirement.

I am not so sure how long his enthusiasm will last, though. He has been late to the party before, standing-back and waiting for the "ideal" market situation, instead of following a steady (and frankly easier) investing strategy. In late 2015 we have again reached price levels that indicate it would be much more prudent to accumulate cash rather or even reduce some positions than be fully invested and take unnecessary risks.

Opposing Forces

There are countless other examples where people made one or two investment decisions that completely changed their lives. Then there are examples of people like Mr. Standingback, who do exactly the opposite, always one step behind and always trying to play catch up with lost opportunities, constantly caught in the harsh investment cycle of buying and selling.

The winners applied the 80/20 principle, whether consciously or not. The losers didn't.

The extreme winners are what I call "Super 80/20 Investors."

They focused on the 20% of the 20% of the 20% of the 80/20 principle, meaning that a single investment decision brought them 99% or more of their lifetime investment returns. Compare this to professional and conventional investors, such as Standingback, who feel forced to make decisions continuously just to catch up with their losses or feeling pressured to make use of their cash.

Some of them feel the urge to make several trading decisions a day, every working day of the week, with no guarantee that more trading will actually improve their investment performance. On the contrary, they create unnecessary trading expenses, increased tax payments, and much more admin work for themselves. Not to mention that additional stress when positions traded at substantial losses.

At this point, I would like to mention that I am not a proponent of what investors call "buy and hold forever" strategy, nor am I opposed to it. I don't want to suggest that you should be looking for that holy grail of investing, the next Apple or the next Facebook (even though that would be awesome). I am showing you these examples to demonstrate that very few decisions, and hence very little work in investing, can have an impact on your lifetime success, a success which professional investors with their busy day jobs and complicated theories can only dream of.

Developing an 80/20 investment approach

So how can we develop an investment approach that actively makes use of the 80/20 principle to investing? First, we will have to decide on what Koch calls "an 80/20 destination." In this process, we have to determine the type of individual investor we truly can be and what fits our personal lifestyles. You will find answers to the questions, how the 80/20 principle to investing works, and whether you should mirror the work activities and daily habits of professional investors.

We will apply an analytical approach to investing, so that we can identify those tasks that generate most of the outcome. As a result, we will be able to focus our energies on the 20% that simplifies the whole process of investing, in order to attain our set 80/20 destination.

Finally, you have to take action. Systematically, you will learn how to execute all the points we have identified as the most valuable tasks and procedures by adjusting the investment process to your own circumstances and personal lifestyle.

To give you a convenient overview and an easy-to-follow concept, I will spell out Koch's simple three-step process [6]:

Step 1: Decide on your 80/20 Destination

Find out what type of investor you want to be -- a Conventional Investor or an 80/20 Investor. A Standingback or Womack? A day-trader who trades several times a day every day or an Investor who only does cherry picking with the occasional investment every other year. Your decision has to fit your personal lifestyle and meet your return expectations. In the end, the goal should be that investing contributes to your financial freedom in the easiest, least risky, and least work-intensive way.

Step 2: Find the 80/20 route

Analyze and compare conventional investment approaches to methods used by successful investors who make use of the 80/20 principle. By identifying the easiest way to our chosen destination, we will extract the tasks representing the most positive outcome, and with these in mind, we will be able to create a tasklist of action points to reach our 80/20 destination.

Step 3: Take 80/20 actions

The final step is vital. This is when you have to take specific actions. You will implement the key tasks identified in step 2, and you will learn specific action points to become the investor you have chosen to become in step 1. There will be real-life examples and case studies to clarify each action step. It will be up to you to choose the 80/20 path and to take action.

Set your destination

If savings and investing is the 80/20 way to financial freedom, attaining happiness, and regaining power over our lives, then saving and investing the 80/20 way should be the ideal approach.

Your 80/20 destination should be clear and simple. With the least amount of work effort and a minimum amount of risk, we want to achieve adequate investment returns in order to have plenty of time for those activities that are truly important to us. Investing the 80/20 way should support our overall goal of achieving financial freedom and laying the foundations for our desired lifestyles.

Before we set the parameters for all three steps though, we need to clarify and understand a few key principles. We need to understand the principles of money, investing, and risk--the pillars of 80/20 Investing--so that we have a better understanding of the whole 80/20 concept to investing in later chapters.

PART II:
LAYING DOWN THE FOUNDATION

CHAPTER 4:
Understanding the principles of Money, Investing and Risk

In 1785, a French mathematician named Charles-Joseph Mathon de la Cour wrote a parody of Benjamin Franklin's *Poor Richard's Almanack*. He called it *Fortunate Richard,* and it aimed to poke fun at the entrepreneurial spirit and American optimism represented by Franklin. In his piece, the Frenchman wrote about its hero, Fortunate Richard, leaving a small sum of money in his will to be used only after it had collected interest for 500 years.

"Fat chance someone would be dumb enough to try that. Ha. Ha."

Franklin, who was 79 at that time, wrote to the Frenchman thanking him for a great idea and telling him that he had decided to leave a bequest to his native Boston and his adopted Philadelphia. When Franklin died in 1790, he left a gift of $5,000 to each of his two favorite cities. He stipulated that the money was to be invested and could be paid out at two specific dates, the first, after 100 years, and the second payment 200 years after the date of the gift. After 100 years, each city was allowed to withdraw $500,000 for public works projects. After 200 years, in 1991, they received the balance—which had compounded to approximately $20 million for each city.

Even after his death Franklin's lesson to future generations about the power of compounding interest becomes clear. As Franklin himself liked to describe the benefits of compounding interest, "Money makes money. And the money that money makes, makes money." [7]

Principles of Money: What is compounding?

Pareto's classic observation started how land was distributed in his own native country of Italy? He showed that approximately 80% of the land was owned by 20% of the population.

Today, a small percentage of the global population enjoys 80% of the wealth worldwide. According to the International Monetary Fund (IMF), the total gross domestic product of all 196 countries in 2011 was US$79 trillion.

Of this amount, over US$63 trillion come from just 22 countries. This means that 80% of the world's wealth is concentrated in just 9% of the countries.[8] We can observe the same phenomenon of the distribution of wealth among individuals where according to OXFAM "62 people own the same as half the world" [9]

The causes for the unequal distribution of wealth, whether among countries or among individuals are manyfold and complex. Leading experts and economists have a multitude of explanations with almost all disagreeing with each other. What is however, undeniable by all of them, is a natural phenomenon called "compound interest", which is a driving force for all accumulation of wealth. It is vital that every private investor understands the power of compounding.

Basically, money underlies the law of "compounding"-- according to popular belief, the "most powerful force in the universe". It is an invisible power that moves masses, including money, in a nonlinear fashion. Money attracts more money, seemingly without any outside input of energy or labor. Like Franklin's gift to Boston and Philadelphia, that was never touched, but paid out ridiculous returns because it rode out the seasons of highs and lows.

Those who observe compounding interest keep on getting richer, while those who ignore it will never achieve their financial goals, or worse, they'll remain poor. According to Richard Russell, author of the Dow Theory Letters, "He who understands interest -- earns it. He who doesn't understand interest -- pays it." Those who don't understand this principle become slaves to money rather than masters of it. Those super rich you read about in the Forbes Rankings surely understand the power of compounding.

Compound your money

The magic of compound growth can generate cash flow that far outperforms any salary an average employee could earn in a lifetime.

One of my most favorite articles on investing is "Rich Man Poor Man" by Richard Russell.[10] In this short article, he describes compounding as the "royal road to riches, that is simple, safe and easy to do."

Furthermore, he explains that perseverance and discipline are necessary to continuing on the compounding route, because the whole process takes time. One must keep on saving and keep on reinvesting the proceeds. To really comprehend the power of compound interest, we need to have a look at some simple compound tables.

Figure 4-1: Family Investment Plan @ 10%

Year	Yearly Contribution	Interest Income	10%
1	2,000		2,000
2	2,000	200	4,200
3	2,000	420	6,620
4	2,000	662	9,282
5	2,000	928	12,210
6	2,000	1,221	15,431
7	2,000	1,543	18,974
8	2,000	1,897	22,872
9	2,000	2,287	27,159
10	2,000	2,716	31,875
11	5,000	3,187	40,062
12	5,000	4,006	49,069
13	5,000	4,907	58,975
14	5,000	5,898	69,873
15	5,000	6,987	81,860
16	5,000	8,186	95,046
17	5,000	9,505	109,551
18	5,000	10,955	125,506
19	5,000	12,551	143,057
20	5,000	14,306	162,362
21	10,000	16,236	188,599
22	10,000	18,860	217,458
23	10,000	21,746	249,204
24	10,000	24,920	284,125
25	10,000	28,412	322,537
26	10,000	32,254	364,791
27	10,000	36,479	411,270
28	10,000	41,127	462,397
29	10,000	46,240	518,637
30	10,000	51,864	580,500
	Cash Contribution	**Return Contribution**	**Total Assets**
	170,000	410,500	580,500

Figure 4-2: Family Investment Plan @ 15%

Year	Yearly Contribution	Interest Income	15%
1	2,000		2,000
2	2,000	300	4,300
3	2,000	645	6,945
4	2,000	1,042	9,987
5	2,000	1,498	13,485
6	2,000	2,023	17,507
7	2,000	2,626	22,134
8	2,000	3,320	27,454
9	2,000	4,118	33,572
10	2,000	5,036	40,607
11	5,000	6,091	51,699
12	5,000	7,755	64,453
13	5,000	9,668	79,121
14	5,000	11,868	95,990
15	5,000	14,398	115,388
16	5,000	17,308	137,696
17	5,000	20,654	163,351
18	5,000	24,503	192,853
19	5,000	28,928	226,781
20	5,000	34,017	265,798
21	10,000	39,870	315,668
22	10,000	47,350	373,018
23	10,000	55,953	438,971
24	10,000	65,846	514,817
25	10,000	77,223	602,039
26	10,000	90,306	702,345
27	10,000	105,352	817,697
28	10,000	122,655	950,351
29	10,000	142,553	1,102,904
30	10,000	165,436	1,278,340
	Cash Contribution	**Return Contribution**	**Total Assets**
	170,000	1,108,340	1,278,340

Figure 4-3: Family Investment Plan @ 20%

Year	Yearly Contribution	Interest Income	20%
1	2,000		2,000
2	2,000	400	4,400
3	2,000	880	7,280
4	2,000	1,456	10,736
5	2,000	2,147	14,883
6	2,000	2,977	19,860
7	2,000	3,972	25,832
8	2,000	5,166	32,998
9	2,000	6,600	41,598
10	2,000	8,320	51,917
11	5,000	10,383	67,301
12	5,000	13,460	85,761
13	5,000	17,152	107,913
14	5,000	21,583	134,496
15	5,000	26,899	166,395
16	5,000	33,279	204,674
17	5,000	40,935	250,609
18	5,000	50,122	305,731
19	5,000	61,146	371,877
20	5,000	74,375	451,252
21	10,000	90,250	551,502
22	10,000	110,300	671,803
23	10,000	134,361	816,164
24	10,000	163,233	989,396
25	10,000	197,879	1,197,275
26	10,000	239,455	1,446,731
27	10,000	289,346	1,746,077
28	10,000	349,215	2,105,292
29	10,000	421,058	2,536,350
30	10,000	507,270	3,053,621
	Cash Contribution	**Return Contribution**	**Total Assets**
	170,000	2,883,621	3,053,621

From the tables, we understand that compounding can only work over time. Usually, saving is not very exciting for the first 10 years or so, until it reaches the point when cash from investment returns starts pouring in at a rate that rivals your day job salary. At that point, anyone will become fascinated by compounding money.

We can also see the enormous exponential change in outcomes by just extending our target compound returns. The financial impact from 10% to 15% and then 20% is phenomenal. That's why Mr. Standingback rues the day when he sold his shares for a profit, but missed out on over 30% annualized stock gains on his Apple shares in the past 16 years.

Figure 4-4   APPLE HYPOTHETICAL PORTFOLIO

APPLE Scenario I	APPL
Purchase Price Oct 1998	1.20 (*adjusted price)
Shares purchased	8,300
Invested Capital	$10,000
Dec 2015 Price	105
Total Income	$861,500
% Return	8650%
Portfolio Value Dec 2015	$871,500
Accumulated Cash	$195,000
TOTAL ASSETS	**$1,066,500**
CAGR	**32.2%**

*Compound Annual Growth Rate

How billionaires see compounding

According to *Forbes Magazine*, Bill Gates has a fortune of about $80 billion as of August 2015. He is extremely rich by any standard, but just imagine if he decides to lend all his wealth to the US Government (which is widely considered as the safest form of investing) at an investment yield of about 2.2% (the income yield of 10-year government bonds).

He would receive about $1.7 billion a year before tax for basically doing nothing, just checking his cash portfolio, collecting his interest coupons, and saying hello to his bankers and accountants once a year.

For the fun of it, let's take it a step further.

I'm sure a shrewd entrepreneur like Gates is capable of compounding $80 billion at a higher compound rate than 2%. Add to this some influence from his good friend Warren Buffett, and a 5% before tax compound rate is realistic. That would mean income of around $4 billion annually. No doubt about it, money does attract more money.

Low Interest Environment

Unfortunately, the magic of compounding cash savings has completely lost its charm since 2008, due to extremely low interest rates in leading industrial nations such Japan, Germany, and the U.S.

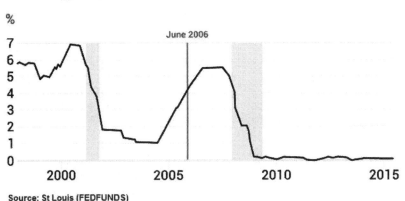

Figure 4-5: Effective Federal Funds Rate

Source: St Louis (FEDFUNDS)

For the time being, all savers, whether large or small, have to be content with almost zero-percent interest rates, or search for higher yielding investments with uncertain returns, price volatility, and higher risks in order to achieve a similar compounding effect. For savers without investment education or experience in investing, this is unfamiliar territory.

Principles of Investing

Investing is a peculiar activity, and there is nothing else like it (except pig farming). More work effort, higher IQs, or better financial education do not translate into better investment returns. On the contrary, if that were true, all Wall Street professionals trained at Ivy League schools with top MBAs or PhDs would outperform all other investors as a whole by a wide margin.

But they don't!

On the contrary, scandals have been well documented over and over again involving all areas of Wall Street. The focus of these scandals range from pure incompetence and gross negligence, to excessive gambling with others people's money and plain fraud, such as insider trading or embezzlement. Bernie Madoff comes to mind. Obviously, perceived intelligence is not enough to replace the character traits necessary to be a successful investor.

Any person with an average intellect can achieve outstanding investment success. Some overly critical folks would even go as far as to say that "a blindfolded monkey throwing darts at a newspaper's financial pages could select a portfolio that would do just as well as one carefully selected by experts."[11] By nature, successful investing is about decision making. Or rather, smart decision making, not complicated decision making processes.

Unfortunately, professors of modern finance don't teach this rudimentary skill. They are much more focused on modern finance theory rather than common sense decision making.

For the purpose of further discussion, let's define what investing really means and what it doesn't. Looking at Investopedia's definition:

Investing is "the act of committing money or capital to an endeavor (a business, project, real estate, etc.) with the expectation of obtaining an additional income or profit. Investing can also include the amount of time you put into the study of a prospective company, especially since time is money."

I prefer Benjamin Graham's definition in the *The Intelligent Investor*: "An investment operation is one which, upon thorough analysis, promises safety of principal and an adequate return. Operations not meeting these requirements are speculative." [12]

According to this definition, there are two components to investing: capital protection and adequate returns.

In investing, "promising safety of capital" demands protecting your capital base at all times. This makes intuitive sense. Aside from saving you sleepless nights, it will help you grow your capital rather than seeing it shrink or disappear. So you better make sure to invest in something that doesn't lose you money before committing your hard-earned cash.

Nevertheless, an investment should also offer an adequate return. You are not aiming for "record double digit" returns, but adequate compensation that makes it worthwhile taking more risk. Nor do you aim for subpar returns you could simply achieve by holding cash or US or German government securities, which are widely considered risk-free investments. We want more money in real terms after taking inflation into account. Here, I would like to emphasize that whether you consider yourself a stock, gold, private business, or real estate investor, or if you only invest for income such as dividends or rental income, all investors in all asset classes have to obey the same laws and principles of investing. There is no exception!

Sometimes, there is confusion regarding what investments really are. Let me make it clear, if you buy an asset and it's costing you money to maintain it - it is not an investment!

There are countless property owners in China thinking they made a killing, but their properties are empty and it is actually costing them money to maintain their empty property. That is not even taking any depreciation and decay of the property into account. There are whole ghost towns in parts of China built in the middle of nowhere, pushed by real estate developers, and supported by regional governments. These are forms of speculation, which project that land and property prices will increase based on the assumption that demand will increase in the future. Up until now, this has not been the case. With falling birth rates, unfavorable demographics and a slowing economy the miracle cities and their properties slowly decay in the harsh environment of China's interior.

The perfect Asset Allocation is not investing!

Another investment myth is that laying out money according to an elaborate asset allocation pie chart is standard and prudent investing. After all, professionals seem to use and promote it. It is not prudent investing! Nor does it protect investors from market variances such as those we experienced in 2008 and 2009. Asset allocation models completely failed. Such methods are akin to placing one's mind on autopilot and not thinking at all, in the hope that one's investment adviser and his perfectly designed pie chart will protect us from declining market prices. Well, it just doesn't work that way. On the contrary, this approach is diversification overkill and limits your real investment potential. You would be better off keeping cash, simple index funds, or just government bonds.

That brings me to another popular misunderstanding. What you do with your money in order to satisfy your urge to gamble and to speculate is your own private concern. But be honest to yourself, and admit that you are about to speculate or purely gamble with your money. Be prepared for the possible outcomes and use only money you could afford to lose, even if your initial speculative trades seem to be successful.

Almost all investors I know, who consider themselves proper investors according to the definition above, like to do the occasional trade, punt on pure speculation. But they do it with money they consider part of their gambling portfolio, or play money. They would never risk their financial well being by mindlessly gambling with their main wealth.

What distinguishes a good from a bad investment?

Good investments can be purchased at prices that generate high returns adjusted for inflation. Ideally, these assets can grow to infinity without hurting their returns, so that a compound effect of money can take place (i.e. are able to reinvest their income at the same rate of return). These investment assets can be businesses, real estate portfolios, and even other investment managers who are capable of compounding money at very high returns consistently after all fees charged.

Bad investments are the exact opposite. They require constant new capital to keep an investment going at ever lower returns, or in the worst case, negative returns - in effect your are burning money.

Finding excellent investments is actually not too difficult, even though they are extremely rare. Everybody knows that very few investments are capable of achieving annual compound rates at 15% or more and actually can deploy more and more capital in the process. But there is a catch. The real issue is that, due to the principle of demand and supply, these types of assets are extremely sought after and hence their purchase prices are so high that it renders their compounding ability useless.

Let's assume you find an investment that can compound $100 at 15% for a long period of time, but everybody knows about it. As an investor, you wouldn't be able to purchase this investment at $100 - you would have to pay much more than that. Due to demand and supply, the market prices would have a price tag more likely of $500. Much higher if a buying frenzy sets in and more investors are chasing for the same investment.

If you paid $500 instead of $100, your real returns would be a meager 3% rather than 15%, because you would get the same $15 (15% on $100) for $500 spent ($15/$500 = 3%), but the hope is that this investment can continue to grow at even better rates. In many cases, this will be wishful thinking or plain speculation. If this investment disappoints in any way, your returns can quickly go to zero or even negative.

Now imagine, for some strange reason, you are able to buy the same investment for $50 instead of the $100 initial asking price, with the same 15% compound return capability. Your returns would be 30% instead of the initial 15%. I am sure you are asking yourself whether these buying opportunities exist in the real world? Believe it or not, financial markets offer these situations like clockwork for reasons we will discuss in more detail in a later chapter.

To summarize, good investors not only find profitable investments like anybody else, but they have the discipline to buy them at prices that will have a high certainty of yielding them at least adequate returns. Lousy investors do the exact opposite.

Principles of Risk

At this point, we need to be aware of what risk means in relation to any investment operation. For any investor, risk represents the chance of real loss. Per the dictionary definition, risk is "a situation involving exposure to danger, harm, or loss." We face the possibility of loss in whatever we buy or invest in.

For investors, the possibility of loss mainly derives from "overpayment risk."

Investing means buying assets, and whenever you buy an asset, you will expose yourself to the risk of paying too much for the value you expect to receive. It is the same whether you buy stocks, bonds, real estate, or part interest in a private business.

In reality, overpayment risk is simple and easy to understand. When you go shopping or buy something on Amazon, for example, you could end up with low-quality goods; they could be damaged, fake, or simply a pure misjudgment of the items use value on your part. What follows is an instant realization that you overpaid for something or that you shouldn't have bought it in the first place - that's classic buyer's remorse. Unfortunately, buyer's remorse doesn't work too well on financial assets as the real valuations are more difficult to assess, and the realization usually comes much later after a purchase.

An investor's misjudgment of overpayment risk can usually be traced back to the following reasons:

1) Greed in the form of wishful thinking, and

2) Incompetence in areas they know nothing about.

Naïve tourists buying souvenirs and antiques in foreign countries get scammed regularly for these two reasons - unfortunately, myself included.

If you don't know what you are purchasing, you are just taking unnecessary risk. If you haven't done your homework to really understand the characteristics of an investment class, you are taking risk.

All too often, it is plain greed and speculative urges that drive a decision to pay for an overpriced asset. It is wishful thinking that someone else will buy it from us at higher prices later on, just because the market is rising and everybody else is doing it. Mr. Standingback was not able to stop investing when the market overheated during the dotcom bubble. The prospect of further easy stock market gains, such as his previous successful investment in Apple, was too luring for him to resist his urges to continue speculating. His investment leading up to the dotcom burst had nothing to do with investment as we have defined above.

On the other hand, Mr. Womack, following his concept of observing the seasons, would have done the complete opposite, or not participated in the tech and dotcom IPO frenzy at all. He would, however, have added to his preferred positions after the dotcom bubble had burst. Mr. Womack invested the same way he ran his farming business, as that is what he knew best. He didn't get lured in by market frenzies, he made big investments then left them alone until he felt it was time to harvest the crop he sowed many years before.

That gave Mr. Womack a decisive advantage. Because he was focusing on his main business of farming he made rational, well thought-out investing decisions. It helped him to stay true to his main guidance, that of observing the seasons. His job didn't allow his emotions to take over, and thus he wasn't influenced by his previous wins and losses, or affected by his future purchases.

Market Risk

In standard finance textbooks and among professionals, the predominant definition of risk is measured by historic price fluctuation. A science has evolved around managing market risk introduced under the general title of Modern Portfolio Theory, initiated by Dr. Harry Markowitz in 1952 with his article "Portfolio Selection." published in the Journal of Finance, vol. 7, No. 1. [13] In Modern Portfolio Theory, the variance (or standard deviation) of a portfolio is used as the definition of risk. It is now considered the determining factor for managing and measuring risk in all branches of finance, investing, and trading.

This definition applies to professionals, but not necessarily to individual investors. The simple reason is that private investors don't manage billions of assets in complicated financial products with leverage and over different time zones and different currencies.

Other types of risks

There are plenty of other risk types you can usually read in financial institutional disclaimers. I dare you to read a disclaimer for a Collateralized Debt Obligation (CDO), or hedge fund investment prospect, without falling asleep or stopping after two pages. It's not fun, and it's extremely boring. You will read something along the lines of management risks, litigation risk, and about specific operational risks, etc. They all have little relevance for the average investor. For developing an investment approach that applies the 80/20 principle, we will focus only on risks that are based on the original definition of risk.

Risk of Financial Leverage

This risk of loss increases exponentially when we add any form of financial leverage, i.e. borrowing money to invest. Whether the investor himself or the underlying investment uses excessive financial leverage, the risk of loss increases dramatically. If you use any form of financial leverage, it is obvious that you add a new layer of risk over your basic investment risks, as borrowed money has to be paid back within an agreed period of time. This makes investment decisions more complicated.

For all passive investors, financial leverage is not recommended and not necessary unless you are buying real estate with a conservative finance plan in place.

Summary

We have set the three pillars of 80/20 Investing understanding the fundamental principles of money, investing and risk. In order to complete Step I, to set our destination and to identify the core 80/20 tasks (see Figure 4-6) we will have a comparison between what I consider 80/20 Investors and modern professional investors (who follow conventional procedures, academic research, and theories.) We will see how both categories handle their investment affairs and how much, or how little, work they need to do.

For this, I would like you to join me on a quick journey through time. We'll consider a short history of investing as well as some noteworthy investors and their strategies who made use of the 80/20 principle.

Figure 4-6: Pillars of Financial Freedom

CHAPTER 5:
A short history of investing and some notable investors

"A person who does not know the history of the last 3,000 years wanders in the darkness of ignorance, unable to make sense of the reality around him"

—JOHANN WOLFGANG VON GOETHE

The three components of money management mentioned in the last chapter were understood and practiced by all successful investors in history. If you study the history of investing, you will find the stories of many long forgotten traders (trading goods) and merchant investors who followed very simple principles, yet were effective and successful.

Historically, investing has always been an individual activity. Today, however, most investment decisions are institutionalized, and there are investment boards that use advisers and consultants. In the past, people saved and made independent investment decisions based on the data they had available. It was only in the last 70 years or so that investing became institutionalized - it even became an academic subject, which today is very often sponsored by the finance industry. However, while scientific research on finance and investing topics has exploded, it has not made it simple or approachable enough for the common person. Instead, all the research and work seems to have just made investing seem all the more difficult, inaccessible, and dangerous.

Handling and investing capital has been a part of human economic activity since before we built our first cities. The Code of Hammurabi is one of the oldest law codes, dating back nearly 4000 years to ancient Babylon. This code deals with marriage, death, and status -

but almost one third is dedicated to creating a legal framework for debtors and creditors in regards to pledging collateral for land and setting up a framework for investing capital. Here is an example:

Ex. Law #265: "If a herdsman, to whose care cattle or sheep have been entrusted, be guilty of fraud and make false returns of the natural increase, or sell them for money, then shall he be convicted and pay the owner ten times the loss." [14]

Even in the age of the old Babylonians, people understood risk and tried to protect their capital. Nothing much has changed, except, on the whole, we tend to use different forms of currency.

Marcus Crassus – 'Golden Life, Golden Death'

"The greatest part of this, if one must tell the scandalous truth, he got together out of fire and war, making the public calamities his greatest source of revenue." Plutarch, The Life of Crassus.

One of the early historic accounts that refers to individual investment techniques comes from Marcus Licinius Crassus (115 BC – 53 BC). You might have heard of Crassus as the man who defeated Spartacus and his slave army in 71 BC. Crassus was not only part of the First Triumvirate of Rome (along with Caesar and Pompey the Great), he was also one of the richest men in the ancient world, and possibly the richest Roman, ever.

Crassus was a shrewd investor and careful spender; his methods were rather dubious by modern standards, but he was certainly never short of a buck. Thanks to Plutarch's Life of Crassus [15], we know some details about his approach to amassing enormous fortunes.

Crassus understood the financial opportunities that war offered for amassing enormous wealth. He supported war efforts by supplying the legions with essential supplies, or just by taxing regions he came to control as governor after successful campaigns. However, his most famous (and effective) strategy was to buy land and all its property at substantially lower market prices from owners who were forced to sell.

Whatever the moral and social ramifications might have been, Crassus understood that the buying price was vital for creating wealth, and he made sure that the buying price was very favorable for him and him alone. His technique brings to mind the expression "fire sale."

Crassus' death was as unique and flamboyant as his entire life. He was killed in the Battle of Carrhae, where historians tell us "that he thereupon had molten gold poured into his mouth to satiate his unyielding thirst for wealth." He died as he lived -- with lots of gold!

Marco Polo – The Trader of Jewels and the Knowledge Arbitrageur

One particular merchant in medieval history stands out as a notable risk taker and investor - Marco Polo. The story of his journey to Asia as told in *Il Milione*, commonly called *The Travels of Marco Polo*, is fascinating and captivating for even today's investor, as it gives not only a detailed account of its hero's travels, but also an account of his merchant business as it developed over the course of his endeavours.

Marco Polo was born around 1254 into a wealthy Venetian merchant family, though the actual date and location of his birth are unknown. His father, Niccolo, and his uncle Maffeo were successful jewel merchants who spent much of Marco's childhood in Asia trading and purchasing rare jewels they sold for a huge profit back home in Venice. Around 1271, his father decided to take him on his next journey east, so that Marco would learn the trade and the foreign languages it required at an early age. At 17, Marco was barely a man, but his father had grand ambitions for their venture to make contact with none other than Kublai Khan, Emperor of the Mongols and of China.

The Polos were primarily jewel traders, but to acquire their wares they traded in salt, furs, wine, and even slaves, as opportunity arose along their journey. Like most merchants at that time, they traveled from city to city and decided on their next destinations based upon the trading opportunities and the political situation. By buying low in one city and selling higher in another depending on specific demand and supply, they were able to gather gold and jewels in the process.

Besides the substantial investments in purchasing goods such as jewels and precious metals, the risks Marco Polo and his family took with their lives were enormous - travel in the middle ages was a very dangerous undertaking. In their travels, the Polos went through war zones, vast deserts, and areas frequented by bandits and raiders in search of the ultimate pay out.

During his time at Kublai Khan's court, Marco Polo and his family amassed a vast fortune in gems and gold. As would eventually become obvious, his knowledge and his accounts would be far more valuable than any jewels or gold he would amass during his 17 years in Asia. Marco Polo died in January 1324, wealthy and successful.

Italy's Bankers

During the same period, we see the establishment of powerful banking clans in Italy's city-states that dominated Mediterranean commerce for many centuries. These 'Merchant Princes' used their banking savvy and knowledge to finance trade and powerful city states in Italy and the surrounding region. But, crucially, they never missed lucrative investment opportunities themselves.

Lorenzo de' Medici (1449 – 1492), the de facto ruler of the Florentine Republic, ancestor of the kings of France, and one of the most powerful benefactors of the arts in the Renaissance, was one such man. His family fortune was built on the power and profitability of the Medici Bank, which his Grandfather Cosimo de' Medici oversaw and grew as one of the leading Banks in Europe, helping the family gain more political influence in the process.

In the same period, Luca Pacioli (1447–1517), who would eventually become known as the father of accounting, is credited with inventing the double entry system of bookkeeping, and he was the first to publish a work on the double-entry system, a system that is still used today and is the basis for all financial reports we can read for researching investment opportunities. He forever changed the world of business, finance, and investing.

The 80/20 Pioneer Investors

We are now entering a period when the term *investor* begins to take on its modern meaning.

The first stock exchanges were established as far back as the 1700s. That was the period when many mercantilist trading companies formed – these companies had stocks that would pay dividends on all the proceeds from all the voyages the companies undertook. These were the first modern joint stock companies. The most prominent and oldest among several similarly formed companies in Europe was The East India Company. It received a royal charter from Elizabeth I on December 31st, 1600, and it was granted monopolistic rights to trade exclusively in certain regions. Wealthy merchants and aristocrats owned the Company's shares, and they made a fortune in the decades that followed.[16]

A century later, the emerging European economy would witness the first major economic bubble in history -- the British South Sea Bubble which grew between 1711 and 1720, and culminated in one of the earliest financial crises ever recorded. The parallels between the Dotcom bubble and the South Sea Bubble are frightening and shocking at the same time. In an environment of relative prosperity, when the British Empire was on its way to rule the world, anything that had to do with overseas trade was a hot investment at that time. This is similar to the situation with tech companies in the Dotcom bubble. The South Sea Company, the company at the epicentre of the South Sea Bubble, was granted a monopoly to trade with South America, even though it was unrealistic that this monopoly would ever make a contribution to its bottom line, due to the fact that South America was controlled by the Spanish Kingdom. The speculation was that Mexicans and South Americans were just waiting for someone to introduce them to British superior manufactured goods in exchange for cargo ships of jewels and gold! In this sheer boom of prosperity and ever growing trade, nobody questioned the the validity of the company's' business model, its management, or the sheer risks involved with trade routes to Latin America. Hence, nobody questioned the repeated re-issues of stocks by the South Sea Company--people just bought the stocks at any price as fast as they were offered in fear of missing out on the next stock price move up that could make investors wealthy overnight. The parallels with the flow of Initial Public Offerings at the peak of the Dotcom bubble are obvious. During the Dotcom craze, nobody checked whether these companies, having names with tech or net in them, actually made money or had capable and honest management.

When news leaked out that the South Sea company's directors and a few investors with access to insider information secretly sold their shares at excessive prices, a full-blown panic broke out. In the same way that everybody wanted the shares at the same time with limited supply, now everything was in reverse - everybody wanted to sell and there were no buyers. It could have been the end of a singular contained company crises, but as usual, there is never only one cockroach in the kitchen, and market participants lost faith in all other company speculations and wanted out. Banks that had lent money to speculators to purchase various stock certificates were sitting on mountains of non-performing loans. The result was loss in confidence in the banking sector, where weaker banks didn't survive the liquidity crises that culminated in a full blown banking crisis in the City of London.

As we know, it wouldn't be the last stock crash or banking crisis. In fact, it was the starting point of many other financial crises, panics, and bubbles for the next 300 years to come.

It was around this time that the first of history's great 80/20 Investors emerged. In the remaining part of Chapter 5, we'll be looking at people from more recent history, and contemporary figures like Warren Buffett. But first, we're going to meet one of the most powerful and important families in the history of finance - the towering Rothschilds.

The Rothschild Family - A Banking Dynasty

Among the earliest and greatest investors who ever lived were members of the Rothschild family from Germany. The founder of this banking dynasty was Mayer Amschel Rothschild (February 23, 1744 – September 19, 1812), a German banker born in the famous "Judengasse" – the Jewish ghetto of Frankfurt am Main. He made a fortune by cleverly positioning himself as the business partner of Crown Prince Wilhelm of Hesse, who became Wilhelm IX, Landgrave of Hesse-Kassel in 1785. Rothschild began by trading in rare and valuable coins. He later became banker to the Crown Prince and other European aristocrats, thanks to his reputation for reliability, trust, and attention to detail.

Rothschild is referred to as the "founding father of international finance," but it was his five sons who realized his vision of an international banking clan operating from the leading cities of Europe. Two sons stood out: Nathan Mayer Rothschild and James Mayer Rothschild.

There are many rumors and legends surrounding Nathan Mayer. One claims that he made a fortune buying in the panic that followed the Battle of Waterloo. Whatever the stories may be, we know that he moved to England in 1798 to set up his own business in textiles and further the family interests in the import and export business. Nathan Mayer became a naturalized citizen in 1804 and established a bank in London.

Nathan Mayer was a very shrewd and experienced businessman and investor. According to Derek Wilson, a leading biographer on the Rothschild family, "N.M. succeeded because he worked harder than his rivals, because he gave his customers value for money and because he was always on the lookout for new markets, new ideas, new ways of doing business." [17]

When entering the Manchester textile market, Nathan Mayer had one advantage over his existing competition -- he was not bound by tradition that was so common among Manchester's established trading guild. As one of the few merchant Jews, he made full use of his advantage of independence and flexibility by gathering into his own hands as many stages of the production and marketing processes as possible, hence streamlining the effort and making it more efficient, and thus generating more free cash flow that he was able to reinvest or invest in new investment operations.

It allowed Nathan Mayer to expand and invest in fields where both he and his family in Frankfurt saw opportunities. His approach was ruthless; legend has it that he once told a colleague to "buy when there's blood in the streets – even if the blood is your own." Nowadays, we might be more familiar with the phrase, "The time to buy is when there's blood in the streets."

When asked how he got so rich, Nathan Mayer attributed his success to two things. He said he always bought when despondency gripped the markets, causing panic and chaos. And he always sold "too soon." [18] He did not wait for enthusiasm to peak. He always knew when to get out, and he got out in time with all his money.

Nathan Mayer had no qualms about benefitting from crisis. He had established himself as such an important banker in the city of London that in the panic of 1825, when the stock market crashed, leading to the closing of six London banks and 60 country banks in England, he was able to supply enough gold coins to the Bank of England to avert a liquidity crisis. He emerged from the crisis not only richer, but with his prestige greatly enhanced. He died in July 1836, and is remembered as one of England's most influential bankers.

Another extraordinary example of investment acumen is the story of Château Lafite under Nathan Mayer's younger brother James. James Mayer de Rothschild was born in Frankfurt (Main) in 1792, the fifth and youngest son of Mayer Amschel Rothschild. When Nathan Mayer moved out to Manchester, and later London, James was sent to Paris, and in 1817 opened De Rothschild Frères - the French banking arm of the Rothschild family.

James was an even more successful banker and investor than Nathan Mayer, who was the dominant brother of the family until his death in 1836. The reason is simple. He outlived his older brother by 18 years.

For compounding money, 18 years is an eternity, which allowed James to far surpass his older brother in accumulating wealth. James was an equally strong-willed and shrewd businessman. He amassed a fortune that made him one of the richest men in the world. Arguably, his most famous investment was the purchase of Chateau Lafite in 1868, just a few months before his death.

In his lifetime, James' real passion was wine. He developed it over many years, becoming an expert not only on rare and excellent vines, but also the business side of it. He was a connoisseur and studied it intensively, even teaching the art and value of good wine to his extended family. He was especially fond of claret, notably the product of Chateau Lafite, which is generally recognized as the leading vineyard of the Haut Medoc in the Bordeaux wine region of southwestern France.

In 1830, eager to secure an unlimited supply, James had tried to buy this celebrated vineyard from owner Sir Samuel Scott, an English banker. The offer was declined. But James was an experienced investor, and not discouraged. He somehow knew that one day his chance would come when he could call himself owner of this one-of-a-kind vineyard. During the years that followed, his interest in the Chateau never waned. He could afford to wait. And wait he did - *for thirty-eight years.*[19]

In 1866, M. Aime Eugene Vanlerberghe - the latest owner of the vineyard - died, and his London bank put Chateau Lafite up for public auction in Bordeaux on July 20, 1868. This was the chance James was waiting for all the years. He bid secretly against a group of British merchants, and finally won at a price of 4.4 million French francs. James promptly renamed the property Chateau Lafite Rothschild. It was indeed a great personal triumph for James. Three months later, he passed away, but the vineyard is still in the possession of the Rothschild family.

The 18th century Rothschild family was the original prototype of 80/20 Investors. They might not have been the first, but thanks to their fame, they were the first to lay down a blueprint for future 80/20 Investors. Both Nathan Mayer and James Mayer were passionate about managing their day-to-day operations as international bankers and business owners.

Both intuitively understood the art of investing, buying low and selling high in areas they understood by heart.

For the Rothschilds, investing was just another tool to solidify their wealth, business interests, and position in society. They were neither obsessed with it, nor were they ever tempted to gamble huge amounts of money where the risks didn't make sense to them. There was never a need for it. They had all the free cash flow coming in from their banking business and their operating business interests. As already wealthy and financially independent bankers and business owners, they had the right mindset for investing. The financial markets just offered them the occasional outstanding investment opportunity to take advantage of, or to be ignored.

The great example of James' Chateau Lafite purchase teaches us another valuable investment lesson: there are not many things we have to do in a lifetime of successful investing. All that is necessary is an eye and understanding for value, and patience - patience enough to wait an entire lifetime for the right opportunity, if necessary.

Hetty Green - The Witch of Wall Street

After the Rothschilds, we come to a time shaped by powerful businessmen, such as Cornelius Vanderbilt, Andrew Carnegie, and John D. Rockefeller. But one person sticks out from these eminent captains of corporate America at the turn of the century, also known as the Gilded Age.

Hetty Green, born on November 21, 1834, was one of the richest women who ever lived. Her reputation as a shrewd investor and hard-fisted business owner led to her being dubbed "The Witch of Wall Street." [20] It is said that many a men fell prey to her "dubious" investment and business practices. Most of her victims were other Wall Street characters less shrewd and capable than her. She was in good company during the Gilded Age.

Green was born into the richest whaling family in New Bedford, Massachusetts, and was trained early on in the arts of financial management and bookkeeping. Part of a Quaker family, she was schooled in money management and frugality. Rather than planning for marriage and motherhood, as the only child of a large business family, Hetty Green had to work early on for the family.

At age 6, Green started reading the newspaper for her grandfather, whose eyesight was failing. Special attention was given to the financial section and she had many conversations with him while learning the trade of market analysis. She recalled that the regimen taught her "what stocks and bonds were, how the markets fluctuated, and the meaning of bulls and bears."

"By the time I was 15," Green said, "I knew more about these things than many a man that makes a living out of them." [21]

Hetty Green inherited an enormous fortune from her parents and relatives. Edward Robinson, her father, died in 1865, leaving her approximately $5 million (equivalent to $77,033,000 in 2015). [21]

Green was a typical 80/20 Investor at a time when no school or university even taught investing. She held to some key principles. Her winning formula for investing emerged in the panic of 1873, which culminated into a full depression. The markets had collapsed and it was littered with financially broken speculators who gambled on borrowed money. From all her cash inheritances she received over the years, Hetty had plenty to pick up the bargains left from the panic selling of 1873.

She concentrated on the obvious growth areas of that time. "Railroads and real estate are the things I like," she said. "Before deciding on an investment, I seek out every kind of information about it. There is no great secret in fortune making, all you do is buy cheap and sell dear, act with thrift and shrewdness and be persistent." [22] Her advice sounds familiar - though she wasn't necessarily looking for blood in the streets!

Green continued cherry-picking bargains, right through the successive panics of 1884, 1890, 1901, 1903, and 1907. "When I see a thing going cheap because nobody wants it," Green explained, "I buy a lot of it and tuck it away.... Then, when the time comes, they have to hunt me up and pay me a good price for my holdings." [22] According to accounts, she only had to wait for the doorbell to ring with desperate sellers to offer her outstanding investment opportunities.[23] There was nothing else to do other than wait, manage her business affairs, read the newspaper, and attend social events.

Green's strategy was pure simplicity: concentrate on your favorite assets bought on the cheap, rarely sell, and reinvest the compounding cash flow. She hardly spent any of her portfolio income; she added it back to her cash and investment portfolio, while maintaining (considering her financial circumstances) a very frugal lifestyle.

When she died in 1916, Green left an estimated fortune of $100,000,000 to her son and some favorite charities - in today's money, it would roughly translate into some $5 billion. [24]

J. Paul Getty - The Playboy and the Oilman

On Monday, May 28, 1962, prices of the New York Stock Exchange buckled under an avalanche of sell orders. The Dow-Jones industrial average plunged nearly 35 points - it was the biggest one-day drop in over 32 years. Crashing through the 600 level for the first time since 1960, it hit a day's low of 576.93. By the end of the day, many blue chip companies traded at prices from 30 to 80% below their 1962 highs. The financial media at that time was quick to come up with attention-grabbing headlines:

Black Monday Panic on Wall Street. Investors lose billions as market breaks nation fears new 1920 debacle [25]

We would need to replace billions with trillions, if those were the headlines today.

By the time they hit the newsstands, hordes of experts and analysts were already offering their explanations, hindsight diagnoses, and gut feelings.

As usual, financial professionals and economists tried to make the most out of the moment by promoting themselves shamelessly, while others enjoyed with "almost sadistic delight" [26] forecasting even worse things to come.

Two days later, several newspapers and TV stations were eager to interview a man who should have been miserable at that time, as his empire must have clearly shrunk and suffered in this financial onslaught -- J. Paul Getty, founder of Getty Oil, and in 1957, named the richest living American by *Fortune* magazine.

When asked what he was doing in light of the recent mass panic selling, Getty answered that, "while he sympathized wholeheartedly with anyone who had lost money because of market developments, he saw little, if any, reason for alarm and absolutely none for panic." As for what he was doing specifically, he answered without hesitation: "I'd be foolish not to buy." [26]

Reporters thought he had gone mad - perhaps due to his old age. What on earth could Getty possibly be buying in this mess? "Oil Stocks!" he said. His reasoning was simple -- since the petroleum industry was the one he knew best, he bought oil stocks. By the end of May, his broker had purchased several tens of thousands of shares in various leading oil companies for his account using cash reserves accumulated from his business operations.

In his interviews, Getty made it clear that he was holding them for the long-term and not selling them for a quick buck.

Fast forward a couple of years, and the outcome was clear. The market recovered quickly. In 1966, only four years later, the Dow Jones Industrial Index traded at about 1,000, and reached new record highs. That same year, the *Guinness Book of Records* named J. Paul Getty as the world's richest private citizen, worth an estimated $1.2 billion (approximately $8.7 billion in 2014). His stock portfolio of oil companies more than doubled by then - an astounding annualized return of more than 18% not counting any dividends, or expressed in a conservative 10% annualized return, he did the investment work for 4 years in advance.

Figure 5-1

J. Paul Getty Portfolio			CAGR
Start	1962	1.00	
End	1966	2.00 (100%)	18.9% (4 y.)

Target Annual Return			10%
No. Years	1962	1.00	
1	1963	1.10	
2	1964	1.21	
3	1964	1.33	
4	1966	1.46	CAGR 19%
5	1967	1.61	
6	1968	1.77	
7	1969	1.95	
8	1970	2.14	CAGR 10%

Compound Annual Growth Rate

In other words, he made 10% annualized returns for about 10 years. Investing the 80/20 way made it possible for him with just a few decisions to generate all the performance we usually aim for, which professional investors trying to mirror in a work intensive fashion day after day, but most of the time with less success.

What was remarkable was Getty's quick decision making. It seemed he spent little work and time making these decisions, but he remained confident and self-assured. His ability to buy in a market environment, where competitors and many stock owners were actually forced to sell, is astounding.

Equally noteworthy is what he actually bought, as he was very frank about it - oil stocks! [26] Indeed, what else do you need to buy if you are the leading expert in oil businesses? He stuck to what he knew and had confidence in his purchases, and that was a key factor in differentiating him from the other investors of the time. The simplicity and efficacy of his investment approach is more than evident.

Henry Singleton - The US Condor

According to Leon Cooperman [27], former Goldman Sachs Asset Management Partner, Henry Singleton of Teledyne may be considered the CEO who has the best operating and capital deployment record in American business.

Henry Singleton was born in 1916. He grew up on a Texas ranch, with the childhood dream of becoming a great businessman like some of his heroes, the great individualists of American history. He began his college education at the U.S. Naval Academy, but finished it at M.I.T., earning three degrees in electrical engineering: a bachelor's and master's degree in 1940, and a doctorate in 1950. After World War II, he joined Litton Industries, an engineering company, where he quickly moved up the ranks to divisional director of engineering by 1957.

In 1960, he and a former coworker founded Teledyne, Inc., with the company's initial funding coming from venture capitalist, Arthur Rock. The first thing that Singleton did was to buy a company that had lost all of its military contracts and was about to go bankrupt. Teledyne got a great deal for the little price they paid, as they were able to get new contracts and build the business up quickly.

What followed was an impressive record of over 120 acquisitions and an extraordinary record of profitability and growth over the course of almost 30 years. Through acquisitions, Singleton built the company from a small enterprise to number 293 on the Fortune 500 list in six years and he moved up the ranks to 22 within ten years. He eventually created a conglomerate of mainly scientific companies, as well as other business interests, such as exotic metals and insurance. Most of these were allowed to operate with very little direction from corporate headquarters.

In 1989, Singleton formally relinquished operational control of the company he had founded and, by then, owned 13.2% of. He resigned the chairmanship in 1991, at the age of 74. He withdrew from corporate life completely, settling down at his massive ranch in New Mexico. Henry Singleton died as he was born -- in familiar surroundings, somewhere close to his beloved ranch in 1999. After his death, his family owned more than 1.5% of New Mexico, plus a 45,000-acre (180 km²) ranch in California.

For the 25 years that Singleton ran Teledyne, the company compounded growth at 25%. Not even modern-day hedge fund managers can do this consistently, over such a long period, and with so little financial leverage.

In comparison to the SP500 from 1963 to 1990, Teledyne returned an astounding 20.4% compound annual return to shareholders, whereas the index only returned 8% for the same period.

Singleton built a record as a manager and capital allocator who, neither his peers nor anybody else in US history, has matched to this day. Amazingly, his general modus operandi was pure simplicity and common sense. He habitually bought low and sold high within his business portfolio, using his own currency or cash from operating companies.

When Teledyne's share price reached historic highs, as was the case in the 1960s, Singleton used Teledyne's overvalued shares as a powerful currency to acquire other businesses. Then when the entire market, and subsequently Teledyne's, share prices fell, he reversed course and adjusted his strategies. Over the eight years that followed, Singleton didn't make a single company acquisition. You need to imagine the faces of his investment bankers; they had been used to getting juicy commissions in sourcing and executing deals for

Singleton, but were now being presented with a consistent "no" to each deal proposition. It must have been a very frustrating experience for them.

Being able to say "no" served a purpose. When Teledyne shares approached historic lows and continued to decline, he no longer needed outside deals, he just repurchased his own shares at very low prices. He knew these purchases offered great long-term value for him and other shareholders. From 1972 to 1984, he initiated a series of buybacks financed from cash and operating free cash flows from various acquisitions he made years before. During that period, he tendered eight times. He purchased shares from his shareholders, thereby reducing the share count (from high to low) by some 90 percent.

By buying his stock back, Singleton shrank Teledyne's capital significantly while maintaining its earnings, hence dramatically improving returns on capital per share. He repurchased stocks when he saw that his own shares were undervalued in the bear market of 1970 and he did it with vigor and decisiveness no investment committee or asset management team could ever do. He purchased them at a price that he, as the CEO and architect of his own conglomerate, knew would give him value - great value. For him, it was obvious.

With the same approach, Singleton dealt with stock investments for his various insurance companies that he controlled through Teledyne and that managed securities portfolios. At the end of the 1968-1974 bear market, he recognized that bonds were overvalued and stocks were undervalued. Accordingly, he directed Teledyne's insurance companies to avoid bonds that anybody else seemed to favor and to accumulate cheap stocks instead. It was not only a unique move among the conformist old boys network at that time, it was a decision condemned openly by the more critical voices within the business community.

For them, it was insane to buy riskier stocks instead of the safe sovereign or corporate bonds. Stocks were deemed riskier due to the recent bear markets' hangover of losses and dismay, when unlucky holders, including liquidating insurance companies, had either been forced to sell at a loss or simply gave up holding stocks altogether.

Singleton was heavily criticized by industry peers and the financial media. On May 31, 1982, *Businessweek* released an article describing Singleton as a lunatic for his stock purchase programs and giving up bonds as safe investments. That was just 10 weeks before the beginning of one of the longest lasting stock bull markets in US history from 1982 to 2000.

Another amazing feats in his approach to managing Teledyne was the complete and utter absence of a business plan. Note that we are talking about a company which made over 120 acquisitions over the course of its history and was ranked in the top 100 of the Fortune 500. This was not a mom-and-pop shop.

Singleton believed, as he later explained at a Teledyne annual meeting, in having the freedom and flexibility to act appropriately in accordance with circumstances rather than the other way around – forcing his view or grand scheme on reality: "I know a lot of people have very strong and definite plans that they've worked out on all kinds of things, but we're subject to a tremendous number of outside influences and the vast majority of them cannot be predicted. So my idea is to stay flexible." [27]

Singleton added, "My only plan is to keep coming to work every day," and "I like to steer the boat each day rather than plan ahead way into the future." [27] That was a time before the internet and globalization, a period which we now consider as less confusing than today's environment.

At the risk of oversimplifying Singleton's approach to managing a Fortune 500 company, we might claim that the lack of a complex and time consuming business plan was actually the competitive advantage allowing for his outstanding performance as America's best capital allocator. With the freedom and flexibility he enjoyed, he was able to divert energies and company resources where they were needed the most and reap the most returns for his efforts. He intuitively followed an 80/20 approach to business management, his business acquisitions, and stock purchase program.

Singleton followed a common sense approach to management by analyzing his role and responsibilities as holdings manager and focusing on only the tasks that were most valuable to Teledyne as a whole.

He neither posed grand visions and centralized business plans on his 120 plus acquisitions, nor did he micromanage them with extreme oversight and control. He simply allocated resources and capital where it was needed the most, depending on current market circumstances. Singleton didn't anticipate or try to predict market moves, he reacted to facts and new situations logically and appropriately -- a very pragmatic approach to management. It would be an unthinkable approach in today's modern area of corporate business plans and centralized control.

In another interview, Singleton said, "I define my job as having the freedom to do what seems to me to be in the best interest of the company at any time." [27] He utilized the 80/20 principle in managing his operations to the utmost advantage and he indeed was America's best capital allocator and the US condor.

Warren Buffett and Charlie Munger - The odd couple

"Be dead right about the big decisions - every investor ought to have a lifetime decision card with just 20 punches. What I try to do is come up with a big idea (gorilla) every year or so. Charlie and I decided long ago that in an investment lifetime, it's just too hard to make hundreds of smart decisions. That judgment became ever more compelling as Berkshire's capital mushroomed and the universe of investments that could significantly affect our results shrank dramatically. Therefore, we adopted a strategy that required our being smart - and not too smart at that - only a very few times. Indeed, we'll now settle for one good idea a year." --Warren Buffett

Warren Buffett and Charlie Munger of Berkshire Hathaway attribute their success to being right on a few big decisions. Both intuitively understood that only very few decisions and very little actual work will make or break a lifetime of investment success.

Buffett's idea of an actual physical punch card to limit investor decisions forces investors to be very selective. He suggests that under the rule of the punch card, investors would really think carefully about each investment decision and would commit appropriately when they made a single investment. This policy may sound overly simple, but nobody can deny its effectiveness, as it maximizes returns and minimizes work and fees.

Indeed, how can a two-man team with a staff of just 24 in 2014 from an office in Omaha, Nebraska manage a financial empire of $526.186 billion in assets without the help of legions of financial advisors, lawyers, and investment bankers, and still outperform the market by a wide margin?

Most people are familiar with Warren Buffett and Charlie Munger, but especially with Buffett. Worldwide, people know him for his folksy advice and common sense approach to investing. Amazingly, though, only a few really follow his advice.

Even today, we hear many people arguing against their success. Some call them a mathematical anomaly, dice throwing monkeys who always win by pure accident, even though it has been demonstrated that there is a growing group of investors with similar performance track records using the same principles. Buffett himself published an article titled "The Superinvestors of Graham-and-Doddsville" that is based on a speech he gave at Columbia University to prove that fact. [28]

Others claim that Buffett always had unfair advantages, always getting better deals than the general public. The most prominent Buffett critic in this camp is Michael Lewis, author of Liar's Poker and Flash Boys, who considers Warren Buffett a hypocrite. But if you studied Buffett's and Munger's career carefully, you would know that it had been a long and very laborious way for them to get into a position to negotiate favorable private transactions. Even Lewis can't deny Berkshire's long-term performance track record.

If you had invested $1,000 in 1964, trading at $19, it would be worth about $11 million today, based on a closing price of $200,000. If you had invested even earlier in his Partnership from 1958, the track record would be even more impressive. When Buffett invested in Berkshire Hathaway the first time in 1962, he got shares for less than $8 each.[29] The stock traded at $200,000 in October 2015.

More impressive is Buffett's company track record as measured by return on capital, or in his case, book value increase per share. According to his latest annual report, since 1965, Berkshire's book value has increased by an astounding rate of 19.4% annually. That is an overall gain of 751,113% measured from 1965 to 2014. By comparison, the S&P 500 index, a benchmark representing the US economy, only increased by 9.9% annually or 11,196% over the same period.

A vital skill, which the investing pair have repeatedly propounded in interviews, is the ability to say "no." It has protected them from many stupid decisions and it has clarified their investment work by actually reducing it. Buffett's most impressive decision to say "no," and the decision that laid the foundation for him being called the "Oracle of Omaha," came in 1969.

Between 1956 and 1969, Warren Buffett managed money in private partnerships. Even though he loved the game, he knew when to stop and he knew when to say "no." He stopped managing money for others in 1969 to focus entirely on managing Berkshire as CEO and Chairman. That was right before one of the most vicious bear markets in US history. It was an amazing feat in today's money management industry and involved amazing timing, not because he actually tried to time the markets, but because he realized there were no longer any opportunities to invest on his terms.

Where professional money managers continued and felt they had no other choice than to continue buying, because that was the job they were getting paid for, Buffett had the courage to say "no" publicly. His decision to resign from professional money management followed as a logical consequence of his own observations. [30]

Charlie Munger took a similar route, but 6 years later. He was hit hard in the bear market of 1973 and 1974 when his partnership lost 31.9% and 31.5% respectively. One investment partner couldn't take the horrendous book losses psychologically and cashed out at the worst possible moment in 1974.

What the client saw following his own fateful decision must have been even more devastating.

Munger's partnership rebounded strongly in 1975, rising 73.2%. Not impressed and deeply upset by this experience, Munger closed his partnership, left the business of managing other people's money, and became vice-chairman of Berkshire the same year. He never looked back.

During the period where Munger experienced his investment "Waterloo," Buffett must have seen his friend struggle with some distress, but also with astonishment. We now know that Buffett readied himself to get back into the market. He was urged on by his knowledge of his friend's investment portfolio, which he knew was trading at unprecedented values. In an interview with Forbes in late 1974, he was asked how he felt about the terrible market situation. His answer: "Like an oversexed guy in a harem....This is the time to start investing." [31] At that time, even a blind person must have seen that Munger's holdings reached "super bargain" price levels, if you knew a bit about these holdings.

Buffett did, and he did the only sensible thing, which was to buy in loads with the cash he accumulated over the previous four years. Naturally, he bought all the stocks and businesses he understood, knew for a long time, which he was dead certain were "super bargains." Why invest in something new when you have all the old investment ideas just lying in front of you?

Many books and articles have been written about Buffett and Munger, and rightly so. They represent the ideal 80/20 Investors who openly display and describe their modus operandi for everybody to copy. Buffett is frequently quoted as "tap dancing to the office," and

Munger is typically seen reading or hanging out with his family and friends, and taking the occasional fly fishing trips.

There is no need for them to impress anybody, especially bankers or outside investors with fancy offices or corporate perks. They don't have to appear overly busy with schedules filled up for three months in advance.

Buffett's office building has the typical charm of a provincial building that has seen its prime a long time ago. It has been located far away from the gravity of finance in the middle of nowhere since he moved his partnership from his bedroom in 1962. "You can think here," he says, "you can think better about the market; you don't hear so many stories, and you can just sit and look at the stock on the desk in front of you. You can think about a lot of things." [32]

Buffett reads what he likes to read, he works and meets with people he likes to meet and work with. He is always unruffled. And even though he eats like a young bachelor, with his regular cheeseburgers, cherry cokes, and T-bone steaks, he has reached a respectable age of 85 and he doesn't seem to slow down, if, that is, we can say he was ever really in a rush.

Conclusion

The list of historic 80/20 Investors could go on and on, and most investors I have presented here are from the past, and are less famous for their investment skills rather than their business acumen.

It proves that successful investing has been done for centuries without the need for financial theory or expensive hardware and software. They all followed some simple principles in investing, and they didn't over-complicate things or make their investing work-intensive. In fact, they too, seemed to obey the seasons for their investment operations. They were all individuals who acted independent of professional advice and of the general market consensus.

It is now time to have a look at the other side of the investing world. The dominant world of modern day investment management, as practiced by professional money managers, investment bankers, and investment researchers today.

CHAPTER 6:
Modern Day Investing

"My experience with very bright and articulate investment managers is that their skills at analysis and logical extrapolation are very good, often super, but that their brilliance in extending logical extrapolation draws their own attention far away from the sometimes erroneous basic assumptions upon which their schemes are based."

—CHARLES D. ELLIS

You have seen several historic examples of great investors and their simple, common sense approach to investing. Modern investment textbooks, university courses, and financial media, however, promote a totally different approach.

Knowing what elements of modern investment management are effective, and which are less effective, allows us further insight into which type of investor you want to be (your 80/20 destination) and can apply to your chosen lifestyle

You also need to understand that banks and fund promoters press their sales and investment processes onto the average individual investor to influence their investment decision making. Once you have seen the whole investment process used by professionals, we will compare the results with the approach of our previously mentioned 80/20 Investors.

Let's analyze a conventional investment process from the beginning. This is the point, typically, when you enter a bank to solicit investment advice on a potential investment decision from professional money managers. Don't worry, I will not bore you with too much financial theory or financial jargon. I will keep it short and simple.

Say hello to your Banker

When you enter a local bank branch, a friendly banker will call you into a quiet area so that he or she can discreetly analyze your current financial situation, income, age, and financial goals. By asking you a lot of questions, the bank wants to make sure to offer you the best individualized investment solutions, although more cynical voices would say that the questions are actually intended to ensure the bank protects itself from potential lawsuits, or how some industry insiders refer to it as, "to cover the bank's ass in case something goes wrong." [33]

Based on your answers, they will assess and set financial targets such as your return goals, investment horizon, and risk profile (whether you are a high risk, medium risk, or low risk taker). Then, they will devise an investment matrix to offer you the appropriate financial products.

The most important step in the whole procedure will be the asset allocation decision based on your answers to the questionnaire. This process divides your investment into asset classes that are considered appropriate for your risk profile, determined by your adviser. The adviser adjusts the percentage of each asset class in your investment portfolio according to your risk tolerance, goals, and investment time frame. In investment management, assets are considered a group of securities with similar characteristics and behaviors, which fall under the same securities regulations. The traditional three asset classes are equities (stocks), fixed-income (bonds), and cash equivalents (money market instruments), but today you will see real estate, commodities, venture capital and even art as asset classes.

Because the average investment of retail investors is small, investment advisers will usually push for funds as a replacement for single securities investments. Their argument is that, this way, you get more risk diversification, have a wider choice of asset classes, and the expertise of selected investment professionals.

Figure 6-1: Typical Asses Allocation Chart - Balanced Portfolio

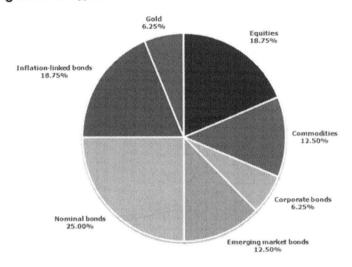

Portfolio's target weights

Often, you will be presented with a pie chart depicting how much you should be allocating in each asset class, starting with default asset allocation models where you put the majority in bonds and the remainder in cash, stocks, or real estate. In recent years, they have been adding precious metals, emerging markets, and even art to the asset mix.

Now, it starts getting kind of complicated. (Yes, it's actually been pretty basic and easy for an investing professional up until now!)

In each asset class you can pick from various third party funds and in-house products. For example, if your bank were Citibank, they would offer their own asset management fund products under the Citibank brand. However, to give their customers a wider choice of asset classes and fund products, they could be offering funds managed by leading investment management brands such as Pimco or Fidelity. Of course, you usually pay all required fees upfront, including any commissions or fees for buying third party products. Bankers don't work for free.

There are different investment philosophies and approaches for each asset class and each investment fund, which depend on the company's marketing strategy and latest trends of products that have been selling well. These could be as simple as US equity funds that only buy and sell in plain vanilla stocks listed on major US stock exchanges, or they may be more exotic funds that guarantee your invested capital, but cap your return potential. Trust me, you don't want to know more details.

You can see where this leads to. My head is already spinning just writing about it. It was estimated that in 2012, there were about 4,600 equity [34] funds alone, with an average 7% termination rate - i.e., the number of funds that ceased to exist by the end of the year.

Add to this fixed income funds, hedge funds, and multi-fund management products and you will quickly notice that there might be as many funds as there are individual stocks listed on exchanges.

Recently, Goldman Sachs Asset Management decided to close down its famous BRIC fund that invested in Brazil, Russia, India, and China. The nine-year-old fund lost 21% in the last five years, leading to investors fleeing in droves. According to a Bloomberg report, the fund will be merged with a broader emerging market fund officially sealing the demise of an investment pool that was all the rage not too long ago.[35] Retail investors who jumped on the emerging markets and BRICs bandwagon a bit too late lost a substantial amount of money. At least they can say they had a very popular and prestigious Goldman Sachs fund in their portfolio at one time.

This all seems overwhelming. I promise, we're almost to the part where I show you the smarter and easier way to avoid all this swirling information. It's important you understand at least a bit about the traditional investing industry and practices to understand where you can leverage 80/20 Investing to gain greater returns and save yourself a lot of headaches.

Professional Fund Management

Since 1952, with the introduction of modern portfolio theory by Harry Markowitz, academic research on finance has seen explosive growth in financial theory and product innovation.

Today, all professionals in the finance industry are trained in modern portfolio management, efficient market theory, economic theory, and sophisticated business valuation models. Add to these such subjects as risk management, financial regulation, and ethics, and we have a complete masters degree course that is taught at business schools today to anyone who wants to work on Wall Street.

The professional work of management can be split up into searching for and researching economic trends and companies, followed by administrative tasks such as bookkeeping, portfolio rebalancing, tax filings, and other paperwork. Add to this the work of professional marketing and fund distribution experts that promote their products, and we can easily understand why there are large industries like these in financial centers such as New York, Boston, London, or Singapore.

Newer types of jobs derived from risk management and compliance departments have seen a steady rise in manpower since the subprime crises. At professional investment companies such as Fidelity, BlackRock, or Janus Capital that manage billions, there are specialists for each of these categories, with front office people such as fund managers and analysts enjoying the most prestige due to their direct influence on investment performance. But there are whole armies of back-office staff, responsible for everything from simple paperwork to maintaining all electronic systems.

The fascinating world of professional money management

Generally, the key people involved, analysts and fund managers, perform economic analyses, which consider the broader economy factors followed by detailed industry and single company research. They apply fundamental research using a company's financial statements, or they apply sophisticated technical analyses to study historic price trends alongside a variety of chart studies.

The main job of both buy and sell-side analysts (investment fund analysts vs. broker analysts) is to collect all relevant data in accordance with the fund's prospect or research philosophy, and to create sophisticated spreadsheets with enormous amounts of data, tables, and charts.

The heart of every analyst's spreadsheet is his or her own "forecast engine" that projects future economic trends or company earnings ranging from 4 years to sometimes 10 years into the future. This is a "black box" for outsiders and it's contents are a well guarded secret. Even though the analyst's forecasts look very much like the company's own earnings guidance, leading analysts swear by their own forecasting techniques. Naturally, they want to create an aura of complexity in order to convince their clients of sophisticated added value.

There are also all sorts of research specialists just focusing on monitoring Central banks or global economic data. There are specialists just for certain industries, and specialists for marketing fund products. There are specialists for everything. All analysts interview hords of economists, industry experts, outside analysts, and strategists, including company CEOs, among others.

They attend analyst and fund manager conferences, visit work facilities, and try to network with peers while promoting their company and funds on Bloomberg or CNBC media. In between, they add collected data to their valuation models and write lengthy reports. Sometimes they compose these reports themselves, but sometimes they are written by junior staff or simply copied from other analysts. It's a busy job that can easily take 60 to 70 hours a week, much more if they keep reading reports from other experts in the field on weekends, which they usually do.

Fund Level - The decision makers

On a fund management level, many managers add their own research on top of what they either receive from their in-house or sell-side analysts working for investment banks. They, too, use complex spreadsheets or third-party software, but they mainly use these tools to balance their investment holdings in accordance with some high-grade, in-house risk parameters that are mainly based on the historic price volatility of each holding and their price correlation among other holdings.

All managers carefully monitor their cash positions, their investment exposure to certain industries, and they constantly watch their deviation from their respective benchmarks. If anything moves against their own investment rules or self-set risk parameters, they add stocks or sell positions in bundles to balance the portfolio.

This usually happens on a daily basis, providing work and commissions for sell-side brokers. Don't forget that each fund usually has hundreds of different investment positions, in different stock names, and can be worth hundreds of millions US$. The largest actively managed mutual fund was valued over $110 billion in 2014 [36].

It's like sitting in front of a panel at a nuclear power plant or at NASA mission control. Any outside market change or manipulation of different equity weightings can decide underperformance or outperformance at any point of time.

Fund of Funds (Multi-Manager Funds)

Over the last two decades, the use of multi-manager investment funds has become popular among private and institutional investors. These are funds that don't manage single asset classes, but actually invest in various funds that manage specific asset classes. Instead of buying stocks or bonds directly, these multi-fund managers select other fund managers who make the investment decisions in their respective funds. So there is you, your investment advisor, who only recommends Multimanager funds that invest in fund managers, who finally invest in single stocks or bonds. That's what I call a great money making pyramid!

Comparing Fees

Figure 6-2a: CONVENTIONAL INVESTMENT CLIENT

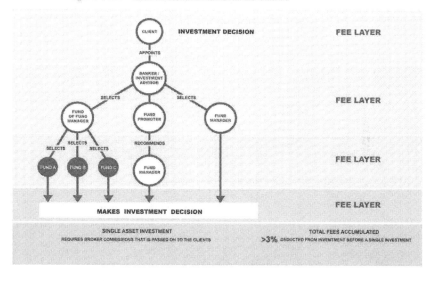

Figure 6-2b: 80/20 INVESTOR

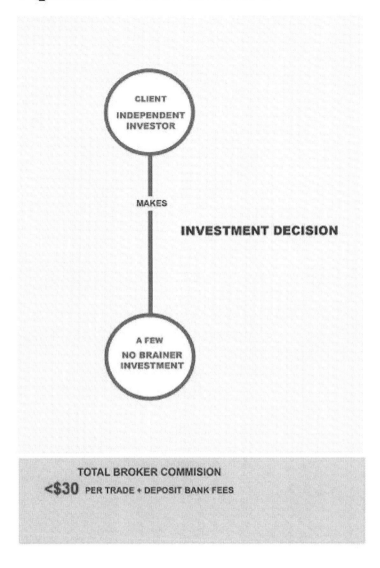

Don't forget, we have fees involved on each hierarchy level before a single dollar of your investment is actually working for you. The theory behind multi-manager funds is that you won't be able to pick the best performing fund and the best fund manager at all times, due to different market strategies that perform better or worse in different market conditions.

This fund subculture has developed its own industry standards and due diligence procedures for finding the top rated fund managers. Their promotional prospects tell us that, as a sophisticated investor, you should diversify in case one strategy or one fund doesn't perform well. Indeed, why not add another layer of diversification and administrative cost over the already well diversified funds and their own fund fees? It can't hurt to scoop up some more fees in the name of asset protection and reduced volatility!

Investment Professional don't come cheap

Now imagine, on all levels, these people need to be paid, and these types of jobs are not blue collar jobs that pay $35,000 a year or less. These jobs are still very popular among new graduates and MBA students - fetching average salaries of $85,300 [37], even at entry-level analyst positions, and "the sky's the limit" for more senior staff. Their salaries are paid out of earnings generated from fees paid by clients, who often receive sub-par returns or even worse.

The professional money management industry operates under a great deal of pressure. The fight for highly valued clients, such as pension funds or high net worth individuals, is fierce. Frankly, most financial services and investment funds are de facto commodity products and only distinguishable by different marketing budgets.

Lousy results for sophisticated work and infrastructure

The investment industry defines its sole purpose for existing as the outperformance of the general market's financial indices such as the Dow Jones or the S&P 500 index, numbers which are derived from the combined performance of the nation's leading publicly traded companies.

Unfortunately, study after study has shown that actively managed funds underperform their respective index funds. In simple terms, you could have bought a cheap index fund any time of the year at any time over the last 20 years and you would have outperformed 80% of all actively managed funds at much lower fees. There are only a handful of actively managed funds that consistently outperform their indices over a long period of time after fees that are usually 1% and up compared to 0.15% for plain index funds. And don't forget the sales commission by fund distributors such as banks or internet fund marketers, which will be withheld from your initial investment in funds.

According to these studies, the most sensible decision to get investment exposure in the U.S is to buy a simple index fund that has generated less than 7% over the last 10 years, at least for US stocks. Of course, many people have been ignoring that advice as they consider index funds boring commodity products.

Thanks to clever marketing, a majority of individual and professional investors are still convinced they can pick the best fund manager with the best outperformance. Naturally, no active manager will ever admit the high possibility of underperformance. The result is that investors in fund products hop from one actively managed fund to another, trying not only to time markets, but also to foresee the next hot fund manager or hot strategy.

Professional fund managers love these clients, because they have been financing their generous paychecks for decades for average performance or even worse performance results.

Chapter summary

The investment management industry and its entire ecosystem of supporting services, has truly seen astonishing growth and sophistication over the last 60 years, with operational structures that are second to none. Their technological resources and human manpower is astonishing and intimidating at the same time. Yet, they are not capable of achieving adequate returns for all the fees they charge, failing to beat their own set benchmarks most of the time.

Still individual investors strive to be like their chosen role models among professional superstars they read about, and aim to mirror their work procedures and habits. Due to aggressive promotion of investment products and their star managers in banks, brokerages, and asset management companies, it is very difficult to escape from this environment, which creates complications and an excess of procedures necessary for large operations.

From personal experience, finding a potential investment target and researching one single company can take months of your available time, trying to make sure that you haven't missed anything. In the end, despite how many hours or days you spend on research, you will never achieve 100% certainty about the stock's likelihood of making you money. In the worst case you analysis might be correct, but your timing totally off and you lose a lot of money for all the hard work.

But somehow, professionals and private investors alike love to compete in this game, which only ever has a very few winners, and which some in the industry term the ultimate "loser's game." It's time to make a decision and ask yourself: Play the game by their rules (professionals), or play your own game, with your own set of rules, that follow common sense and have a much better chance of winning. It is your choice!

CHAPTER 7:
Time to make a decision

multum in parvo - Much in little

—LATIN SAYING

From the overview of the 80/20 Investors and how professional money managers spend their working time, we can see that the ratios of time, labor, and resource expenditure vary widely.

Don't get confused by the different investment philosophies you might have heard of. Whether it's called growth or value investing, GARP, social responsible investing (SRI), or behavioral finance funds, it really doesn't matter. It's all marketing mumbo jumbo created by fund promoters and marketers to raise money from investors – in the end we all want more money out then we have initially invested, or in very simple terms "buy low and sell high."

A hypothetical scenario

Let's do a small theoretical calculation based on the 80/20 principle. The purpose is to reverse engineer a traditional approach of investing that will be linked to our prototype 80/20 Investors' approach.

Imagine you were a professional portfolio manager and kept 100 stocks in your portfolio that somehow reflected your common benchmark with different industries and weightings - let's say the S&P 500 index.

After a quick performance analysis, you would realize that 20 stocks contributed 80% of the performance. (In reality, the majority of large buy side firms get ~55% of their calls right, with only one or two large positions making the year) [38].

Out of these 20, you would further find out that only 20% contributed about 64% to the total performance of your portfolio. Hence, this step would further reduce the number of stocks to only four companies. (20% of 100 = 20 stocks; 20% of 20 stocks = 4 stocks)

Because it was a large portfolio of 100 stocks, you would admit that you actually knew only a handful of stocks very well, due to your personal affinity to the industry or your professional background. If you were lucky, out of the remaining four companies, one would be a company you actually knew very well, understood its business model by heart, and had a fair understanding what it would be worth.

You would then quickly realize the reason for its outstanding performance contribution: it is most likely due to great management, combined with a highly profitable business model. You would also understand that when you bought this company, the price was excellent, or at least fair, given its profit potential.

Why is it not possible to buy only one or two companies out of the four remaining stocks that contributed 64% of the performance? That you understood these two companies very well, and recognized that the performance they generated stemmed from their good purchase price, strikes me as a very persuasive approach to investment management.

Combining these two basic insights in your decision making, truly understanding the business and purchasing it at price that make economic sense, typifies the 80/20 way of investing.

This situation is, of course, only hypothetical and it would be impossible for professional investors to adopt this approach for reasons we have already mentioned. Furthermore, it is impossible for fund managers to anticipate when their selected stocks would be appreciated by the market causing stock prices to increase. Hence, the performance of 80% of them has been and will be mediocre at best and after all fees, simply appalling. Out of the few who do beat the averages in one year, 90% of them couldn't do it consistently for several years in a row.

Now some clever readers would claim that with hindsight it is always easy to determine the big performers, but I would tell them this strategy has been applied by all 80/20 Investors in one form or another. These investors do beat the averages consistently over a very long period of time, generating positive annualized returns with only occasional downturns related to market volatilities. These are the few years where they actually add substantially to their investment portfolio, purchasing only investments they know very well and can distinguish with ease whether they trade at bargain prices. In the following chapter we finally go into the details of an approach that, thanks to the 80/20 principle, distinguishes itself from the conventional management through simplicity and effectiveness of its impact on investment performance.

What differentiates the 80/20 Investor from all other professional investors and traders is the efficiency of their decision making process. In fact, the difference between these investors and their professional peers is so wide that a truck could drive through it. This gap distinguishes a person who tap dances to work, farms pigs, or only does activities he or she likes to do, from the investment professional that makes thousands of decisions each year and is constantly under stress and performance pressure.

Professionals are forced to read mountains of research to stay ahead of the competition, forced to develop complex financial models and sophisticated charts, and, most importantly, explain themselves to impatient and demanding investors once a month through newsletters and presentations.

All this keeps them away from doing work that actually contributes to their investment performance.

A sensible choice: Step 1 - Choose your 80/20 Destination

In a competitive market environment, as an individual investor, you could study the global economy, your local economy, or any single company to death and still come to the wrong investment conclusions, as do many professionals.

Ask yourself, as an employed worker or business owner and entrepreneur, do you really have the time and natural inclination to analyze every domestic and international company and business there is?

Do you really have the mental capacity to analyze and structure all those factors that influence our global economy, where even highly trained and professionals do very dissatisfying jobs, including leading central banks? Do you really want to spend most of your day staring at monitors with blinking price quotations and confusingly entangled chart studies?

As an individual investor, there is no chance to compete with the resources of professionals at large multinational institutions, nor do most of us have the luxury of spending a full day managing our investment portfolios. Logically, it doesn't make sense to mirror strategies and concepts that professionals use. On the other hand, there is really no need for individual investors to overcomplicate strategies with technology or with financial products that are expensive, difficult to understand, or worse, not even necessary.

From an efficiency point of view, it's obvious that private investors should privilege the easy approach of investing in accordance with the 80/20 principle.

Based on the findings of the previous two chapters, you can conclude that one only has to do a few tasks right in investment management work. By choosing a particular field and a few investments in advance, and letting the market price come to your price range, you apply the 80/20 principle, rather than researching every single investment vehicle under the sun.

The prototypical 80/20 Investor simplifies the whole investment management process to create a scenario wherein less work effort can generate adequate and, most of the time, outstanding investment returns.

I have a simple and obvious recommendation for you. Choose to be an 80/20 Investor as your 80/20 destination rather than mirroring the work habits of professional and conventional investors or passing on all financial responsible. Investing the 80/20 way will allow you to focus on your personal priorities in life, while maintaining realistic return expectations supporting your way to financial freedom.

But the choice is yours. Some people are uncomfortable going against tradition and professional opinions. If this is you, the next few sections may not be applicable, as you will be working with a investment advisor or analyst, who will make all your decisions and trades for you. Best of luck on your investing journey!

Taking it to the next level: Step 2 - Find the 80/20 route

If you recall the the 3-step procedure proposed by Richard Koch, in step 2 we determine a route that will bring us to our set destination in the easiest way possible. We want to take steps that represent the 20% that guarantee maximum desired results.

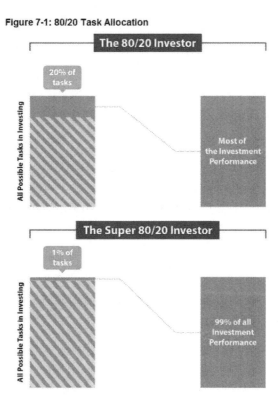

Figure 7-1: 80/20 Task Allocation

Having seen a group of investors who applied the 80/20 principle to investing, we can now present a summary of the specific characteristics they have in common, which we can mirror to follow our 80/20 route:

80/20 Investors are not Traders or Speculators

Among private investors and entrepreneurs, we know that some of us have chosen to become full-time traders. Even in locations such as Bali or in remote areas in Latin America, we find them trading away in front of their laptops. When I am referring to traders, I am talking about people day trading, taking several positions a day, with or without borrowed money, buying and selling tradable products and usually closing their open positions before the market closes, i.e., to sell their positions they have opened at the beginning of a trading day.

Traders try to time all sorts of financial products, such as currencies, commodities, volatility, and recently, even Bitcoins. They apply mathematical models and strategies, and voraciously digest financial news in order to anticipate the next market move, the core component of their decision making process. It requires an enormous time commitment, and has low probabilities of success for the many years spent doing it.

I already hear disgruntled traders protest vehemently. Let me make it clear, there is nothing wrong with being a trader or speculator, and there are a handful of traders who seem to be very successful. But everyone I know, and the traders who are honest with themselves, will admit that being consistently successful in this game is extremely hard. Some studies suggest that 95% of traders lose money, and "only 5% of traders can make a living at it," or "only 1% of traders really make big money." [39]

John Maynard Keynes made a great observation to explain price fluctuations in equity markets and how market participants tried to anticipate market moves. Here is an excerpt from his book, *The General Theory of Employment, Interest and Money* (1936) [40]:

"Professional investment may be likened to those newspaper competitions in which the competitors have to pick out the six prettiest faces from a hundred photographs, the prize being awarded to the competitor whose choice most nearly corresponds to the average preferences of the competitors as a whole; so that each competitor has to pick, not those faces which he himself finds prettiest, but those which he thinks likeliest to catch the fancy of the other competitors, all of whom are looking at the problem from the same point of view. It is not a case of choosing those which, to the best of one's judgment, are really the prettiest, nor even those which average opinion genuinely thinks the prettiest. We have reached the third degree where we devote our intelligences to anticipating what average opinion expects the average opinion to be. And there are some, I believe, who practise the fourth, fifth, and higher degrees."

Even though trading is exciting, with a regular adrenaline rush and great potential rewards, traders have some decisive disadvantages over 80/20 Investors. Day traders are under constant pressure to make money, as it usually constitutes their only source of income. Psychologically, they are in an adverse position from the very start, because they are dependent on markets to trade. Once they stop trading, money stops flowing.

All of the 80/20 Investors we have met so far didn't actually need financial markets to survive. They had money coming in from their business interests, or existing investments, such as stocks, bonds, or real estate.

This represents an enormous psychological advantage that makes all the difference. The standard modus operandi for them is to sit back and wait for opportunities to come to them, because they don't *need* the returns.

All 80/20 Investors operated from a base of financial strength, as they already had all the income they needed. For all aspiring 80/20 Investors, the cornerstone of this approach is to have a solid financial base that supports their current standard of living, as well as their future investment operations. This could come from something as simple as their jobs, their own business, or existing investments.

From a perspective of quality of life, the freedom to use your time as you choose, and financial and emotional stability, makes the path of an 80/20 Investor highly desirable. If you don't want to go through the daily ordeal of trading the markets and having the pressure to earn money on a daily basis, you need to become an 80/20 Investor. If you want to enjoy your life while money is coming in from your chosen day job, businesses, and investments, you should be an 80/20 Investor. If you want to belong to the 20% that understand the principles of money, investing and risk, you need to consider becoming an 80/20 Investor. I recommend all entrepreneurs and individual investors to avoid the traders' path.

The first principle for being an 80/20 Investor: All 80/20 Investors are investors, not traders, or speculators.

Forget about professional investment managers

None of the examples of the 80/20 Investors were the stereotypical Wall Street or Boston investment managers working for large asset management companies. All the investors we have met so far were individually acting investors who enjoyed the freedom and power to make their own investment decisions.

Whether in history or current times, whether in the west or the far east, we always meet individually acting investors. Some of them might work for large multinational holding companies, but the power of decision making is focused on one single person. We have seen Warren Buffett, J. Paul Getty, or Henry Singleton, but these types of individual investors exist all over the world.

For example, in Asia, there are many wealthy business tycoons such as Masayoshi Son of Softbank Japan, or Li Ka-shing of CK Hutchison Holdings, who follow a very similar approach. Like their famous US counterparts, they wait and grasp opportunities when they recognize them.

This habit is not exclusive to billionaires or the super wealthy, though. There are countless private individuals you have never heard of and never will, because they don't get media attention. I personally know a handful of these moderately wealthy individuals, who follow the same strategies. They always accumulate cash and buy cheap when everybody else seems to be selling.

There is really no need to adapt the working procedures and habits of professional investors. The average day of an investment professional can be grueling and is peppered with work they themselves know for certain doesn't contribute to investment performance.

The second principle of 80/20 Investors: All 80/20 Investors are not professional investors.

Why independent investors

The investment and investment banking industry is based on sales commission; therefore, volume is key in the industry's interest - but not necessarily yours. Its primary focus is not to provide individualized and impartial investment advice. Rather, the industry aims to sell their investment products and services, fast and in quantity. The more exotic and complicated the products are, the higher and more opaque their fee structures will be. Selling simple stocks at $5 a trade will not contribute to their bottom line, but selling exotic funds and complicated derivative structures do, as this allows financial service providers to charge higher fees for the added value (as they claim).

This prevalent industry philosophy caused a massive shift from plain vanilla type products and services to sales of complicated financial products with exotic names like CDO, credit default swaps, or knock out warrants, that most professional and individual investors didn't need or didn't actually understand completely.

The numerous scandals and criminal cases we hear in the press are just the tip of the iceberg. It represents the high pressure world of professional investing and finance. Astoundingly, even Ben Bernanke, former chairman of the Federal Reserve, noted in an interview in October 2015 that in the aftermath of the subprime crisis between 2007 and 2009, more individuals directly involved in the crises should have been prosecuted. Few really were.

"I have been uncomfortable with the Department of Justice's prosecution strategy." - " It's not against the law to take a dumb risk. It is against the law to misrepresent what you are selling." [41]

Most investment advisory departments at medium and large commercial and investment banks follow standardized sales pitches designed by product marketing divisions to maximize profits for the time spent on each customer - a kind of conveyor belt approach that has nothing to do with individualized financial advice. In the end, it is just pure economics - just business to them!

All 80/20 Investors we have studied so far never relied on professional advisers for their investment decisions. As they know all too well, more than 80% of professionals fail to beat the markets or sell unnecessary advice and financial products.

Many life tasks can and must be outsourced to professionals and experts in their respective fields, such as physicians, accountants, and lawyers, among others. Unfortunately, it doesn't work that easily for handling your money. Everything related to money management needs to be handled by you and you alone, as the risk of conflict of interest between you and your service provider is so obvious and financially beneficial for anybody who wants to abuse your trust.

Take responsibility for your own money affairs, and that includes investing!

The third principle of 80/20 Investors: All 80/20 Investors are independent investors.

Efficient Risk Managers

"There are two rules of investing.
Rule No.1: Never lose money.
Rule No.2: Never forget rule No.1.

—WARREN BUFFETT

It has been said that the single most important rule in investing is the rule above. I concur! The majority of us have lost money and we know plenty of people personally who have lost substantial amounts in gambling, scams, or from poor investment timing. It doesn't matter whether it was in the financial markets, playing poker, in new business ideas, or even "real estate." We all know the typical phrase we constantly ask ourselves "If I hadn't done this, ...". It's a reflection of our intuitive understanding of what an enormous impact losses have in our quest to achieve wealth and financial freedom.

For most of you, it is obvious that every decision you make in investing and everything that determines investment success comes back to this simple rule, and of course rule No. 2. It may at first sound trivial, but to ensure compounding investment returns, an investor must preserve his or her capital first. Any loss of real capital will diminish your long-term average returns substantially, and it is an enormous psychological downer for your self-esteem, which might keep you away from investing for a long time.

As we have seen in Chapter 4, overpayment risk is the single most important risk in assessing your investment prospects. The relationship between the price you pay and the value you receive is the most important factor in determining your future investment returns. The higher the price relative to what you get, the smaller the potential returns, and worse, the bigger the potential loss.

The fourth principle of 80/20 Investors is: 80/20 Investors are efficient money managers.

Professional Risk Management

Investment professionals apply complicated mathematical risk models based on what they consider the decisive risk in investing - it's called market risk.

Unfortunately, professionals too often confuse different types of risks and make unrealistic assumptions that, in various instances, have resulted in extraordinary losses.

The subprime crisis is just one case in point, and there will be many more to come. Large teams of risk managers equipped with the most powerful technology and software to date were not able to measure or warn of the dire situation they and their institutions were getting into.

The irony of the situation was that almost all investment banks touted their risk management capabilities, and even sold their own risk management products, right up to the end of Lehman Brothers in 2008.

Bear Stearns, which actively sold and promoted their indestructible in-house risk management software "RiskMetrics WealthBench(TM) technology platform" to institutional fund managers and hedge funds, went bankrupt soon after their own sub-prime funds blew up in July 2007, and was finally sold to JPMorgan Chase for $10 a share.

Popular argumentation refers to the complexity of financial products nowadays, their structures as well as the sheer size of the position that spans over the entire globe. In the end, the reasons for their risk management failure were as simple as the end result: human failure and outrageous hubris. There were terrible flaws in risk management based on unrealistic assumptions, classic over-leverage, mixed with plain incompetence by management and fund management alike.

Unlike those investors who brought the recent financial calamity about, all 80/20 Investors we have seen seem to be excellent risk managers, due to a more intuitive and common sense approach to risk. Because of their patient approach of waiting for opportunities, they never took unnecessary risks, and they always stayed within their own field of expertise and training, further reducing it. Besides this strategy, they never used excessive leverage to finance any investments, rather, they used old-fashioned cash to pay for most of them. For Hetty Green, the key was train and real estate assets she acquired knowledge of over many years. For J. Paul Getty, it was oil and oil-related companies, while Buffett chose companies with business models with strong earnings he understood, which he has studied intensively over the years. As for the Rothschilds, they too never bought anything that they didn't completely understand. They never took dumb risks.

The fifth and final principle of 80/20 Investors: 80/20 Investors are smart risk managers.

The ideal 80/20 Investor Profile

From the preceding analysis, we can isolate five points of successful 80/20 Investors to remember:

1. 80/20 Investors are investors, not traders or speculators
2. 80/20 Investors are non-professional investors
3. 80/20 Investors are independent investors
4. 80/20 Investors are efficient money managers
5. 80/20 Investors are smart risk managers

While providing more of what we want more efficiently, the 80/20 route suits the lifestyle of individuals and entrepreneurs who are free in ways that investment professionals and other conventional investors can never hope to be.

The essence of the 80/20 approach:

If we distill all the relevant steps from the previous chapters, we have a good overview that we can use to establish a list of action items essential to becoming 80/20 Investors. Here are the key observations:

- They waited patiently, and accumulated cash in the process.
- They followed intuitive means of risk management because they understood that the easiest way to manage risk was to control decision making by limiting bad decisions, and staying in a field they knew something about.
- By reducing their decision making to a few well-thought out and well-researched decisions, they were able to reduce the chance of mistakes, administrative workload, and transaction expenses.
- They focused on making quality decisions that gave them the confidence in buying or selling.
- They used up most of their cash resources accumulated over the years to have large and concentrated positions, efficiently diversified in different industries or a few single companies.

- They really seemed inactive most of the time, at least in their investment activities. There were sometimes long stretches, sometimes years of inactivity, without any significant purchases or even sales. But they were always looking and always studying potential investments they recognized for their superior economic characteristics, and that they could buy one day in the future.

Your personal action list

With the above list of action items in mind, let's take a deep breath, step back for a moment, and review the whole approach from a passive investor's perspective:

- Accumulate cash from your day job, business interests or existing investments.
- Look at the right places for opportunities, i.e., starting with your own educational background, preferences, and strengths.
- Familiarize yourself with your potential investment targets in advance.
- Act decisively when rare opportunities occur.
- Use your cash, which you have accumulated.
- Continue buying when prices are low or even drop.
- Keep your core position for many years and let the compounding effect work for you.
- Continue reading, studying, and working on your preferred area of interest and expertise.
- Did I forget, continue accumulating cash and wait?

We have found our ideal 80/20 investment route. This is the easiest way to becoming an 80/20 Investor and achieving your financial goals with the least amount of work and energy spent.

This is the most efficient way forward, and it eliminates the need to pay fund fees or other expensive consultancy fees. Usually, inactivity in trading has tax advantages and results in less trading errors as well. Our work efficiency will be much higher due to concentration and simplification.

In the following chapter, it will be time to take action, and to complete step three of the whole 80/20 Investing process. I will outline and describe in detail what level of effort should go in each task from the route.

We will go through the list point for point by starting from cash management and decision making, then discussing how to find opportunities in the right places. Finally, we will find some simple instructions for portfolio management and how to deal with unwanted emotional influences.

PART III: TAKE ACTION

CHAPTER 8:
Set a Primary Cash Flow

"Then he looked at me shrewdly from under his shaggy brows and said in a low, forceful tone, 'I found the road to wealth when I decided that a part of all I earned was mine to keep. And so will you."

—THE RICHEST MAN IN BABYLON

Before you start investing, you need capital.

Most of the investment books you might have read don't talk about where the money you invest comes from, nor do they teach you how you should manage it in combination with investing. For 80/20 Investing, however, it is one of the cornerstones of this investment approach. It is the secret to your structural advantage as an independent 80/20 Investor. Sourcing and protecting investment capital needs to be fully understood before you start to invest.

So where do you get the cash from? All humans have one asset given from birth: time. Investing itself starts early on. You decide what to do with the time given to you by converting it into cash. It's no wonder that people often quote the phrase "time is money", because it certainly is. Time can be converted into money, and it functions as currency in your life.

This doesn't mean you have to be a teenager to start investing, though that certainly would help! If you are reading this book and approaching mid-life, there are still some serious gains and strategies you can put in place to amass a nice return. The point is to get started as soon as you can, whatever that might mean for you.

How do you convert time into hard cash?

Let me give you a short answer: work, sacrifice, and patience. Unless you are rich already or just plain lucky, you need to work and save money, which requires time and sacrifice. Everything starts with a single cash source from which you can establish a capital base, or "cash portfolio," to invest.

There is a time in your life when you should convert time into money. This is typically in one's youth, the earlier you begin the better. Any cash inflow will do, whether it's from a regular daytime job, a private business, or any existing investments that already yield returns. What you study at university or even what you do for a living doesn't really matter. For all I know, you could be a plumber, a student, or a self-employed, location independent freelancer. In any of these situations, you could still beat most high-paying white collar workers to financial freedom, who don't follow the principles of money, and who feel pressured to "keeping up with the Joneses."

Here's a tip, though: for all the work you will be doing early on, converting your time into money, choose an occupation that earns you enough to be able to save even small amounts. It should be an occupation you actually enjoy, or at least don't mind doing. Rather than focusing on a long-term career where you hate the first years of your work life, you should aim for a balance between career satisfaction and savings potential.

There are countless examples of individual investors with average paying occupations or small to midsize businesses who were able to lay the foundations of their financial freedom. In *The Millionaire Next Door* by Thomas J. Stanley [42], you can read about many average income households and simple family businesses that achieved that balance. You have to have a strong desire for this balance, and you have to surround yourself with people who support you in your quest towards financial freedom. Discover a vocation that both satisfies your personal interests and repays your efforts in cash - self-employment, digital nomadism, and entrepreneurship are valid and modern alternatives to achieving your vision of financial freedom.

You don't have to become a lawyer, investment banker, or other high salaried, white collar careerist, unless you genuinely enjoy these types of jobs or have a natural talent and aptitude for them. Choosing a classic white collar route might actually be a riskier choice. Besides the lack of job security, the real risk is that your social circles will always drag you back into a vicious cycle of more work and more consumption. In the end, you will be caught in a classic rat race of more entitlements, perks, and luxury rewards only few can escape.

How to save money

The message from the parable "The Richest Man in Babylon" is simple: "any money you earn a part of, you save for you and you alone." [43]

Saving is the surest way to create wealth. All the 80/20 Investors you have met so far were masters in saving. Many have even been called penny pinchers, but the message is clear: in order to create wealth, one needs to live below one's means.

Applying the 80/20 principle, nothing is easier to execute or has a bigger impact to your savings account than the golden rule of saving: **"Pay yourself first."** Save 10% of your income before you pay anything or anyone else. Although this is a very subtle message, it is most powerful in accumulating wealth.

For every dollar that you earn, 10 cents should go straight to your cash account. This simple technique works because you are tricked into managing your household with a slightly smaller budget and your spending adjusts accordingly. The opposite is also true. If you have a higher salary, you tend to automatically spend more. In the end, you end up wondering why you aren't able to save more.

This 10% of everything you earn is automatically channelled into a savings account that I call a **"cash portfolio."** You can do it either by manually withdrawing cash from your bank account and depositing it into a separate savings account, or you may instruct your bank to automatically deduct 10% from your salary every payday. I prefer the manual way because you can get a real feeling for the flow of money to your wealth contribution.

In some countries such as Singapore or China, citizens and companies alike are even forced to have a high savings rate. In Singapore, for example, employees 50 years and younger have to save 17% of their income. Add to this the 20% their companies have to contribute for their employees social security, and the total savings rate reaches a level of 37%.[44].

That this system of scraping the cream from the top works is demonstrated by governments. Through income tax being deducted before you even receive a penny of your hard-earned cash, your governments make sure they get their cut first, with amazing efficiency.

Recall the stories of Mr. Womack and Mr. Standingback. Both were hard workers and excellent savers, and both were able to accumulate the funds needed for their investments. Even though Mr. Standingback may have been a terrible investor over the last 20 years, he always worked and saved persistently every month, following the golden rule of savings at even higher rates than 10%, driven by his desire to retire early. (He told me it was closer to 50%)

This is a virtue that the younger generation should learn from. Whatever money Mr. Standingback lost in his investment campaigns, he always got back through good old-fashioned savings. Had he just held onto his cash with a little bit of interest, he could be planning his early retirement by now.

Pay yourself first, even if you have loans to repay

That rule also applies to any loan commitment you might have. Even if you have outstanding debt, pay yourself first. Credit card bills, student loans, or mortgages -- it doesn't matter. The main reasons are psychological and not purely financial. You should always have some personal savings to fall back on and to inspire you on your way to financial freedom. If you can't save 10% then start with a lower rate, let's say 3 to 5%, until you have completely paid back your outstanding high interest loans. Afterwards, you can increase it to the default 10% rate.

Should you be able to save more, do so. I personally favor a higher rate, say 15 or 20%, especially in earlier years before you have more family responsibilities, but this is up to you and your financial situation. I know it's difficult to live frugally with all the bombardments of ads, commercials, and social pressures, but I'm sure each of you have the ability and the willpower to cut away some unnecessary consumption, as long as you are motivated to pursue financial freedom.

There are plenty of books and free resources on saving techniques, risk of employment, or increasing income potential by becoming an entrepreneur, among others. In the Bibliography you will find a list of recommended reading.

Secondary Savings Techniques

The following two techniques might have less impact than the "pay yourself first" rule, but they are useful to know nevertheless.

If you shop for something and you have set your initial budget, try to find a similar product or service for a cheaper price. Then, add the difference to your savings account. You are hitting two birds with one stone – you do your spending and consuming and add to your cash portfolio. There are not many ways that let you consume and make you richer at the same time.

The following savings technique is obvious. Simply ask yourself frankly and honestly whether you really need a particular purchase and whether it really supports your life goals. If the answer is a quick "no," forget it and put the money you have budgeted for it into your cash portfolio. Pat yourself on the back for ultimately supporting your life goals. It will motivate you and soothe the pain you might experience by passing on the desired item. It may be difficult to do this at the beginning, but with some practice, it will become easier.

If this approach still doesn't work, use the old Ben Franklin compound technique: "A penny saved is a penny earned!" Ask yourself how much money your consumption would represent, if compounded at a rate of 10% using the "Rule of 72." According to this rule, it takes about 7.2 years to double your money, when divided by the interest rate you wish for.

So if you saved $1,000 today, it would compound to about $17,000 in 30 years. At 20%, it would take only 3.6 years to double, so in 30 years, that would represent roughly $240,000.

That means spending $1,000 today would cost you $240,000 of your future potential money. Is your next purchase today really worth losing this fortune tomorrow?

If you begin your financial life by following the abovementioned techniques, these powerful methods will set you on the path to financial freedom. Combine these principles with the amazing power of compounding, and you have a cash portfolio on steroids.

Don't underestimate the act of saving

As you have seen from Chapter 4, even a small annual savings can make a huge impact on your quest for financial freedom. You can save a decent amount from almost any type of job, if you understand how money works and if you reduce your consumption to appropriate levels. And trust me, you don't have to be a miser like Getty, Green or Buffett.

Recall the compound return table from Chapter 4. The path to financial freedom becomes obvious as soon as the compound effect approaches amounts that equal the money you need on a yearly basis. Your savings contribution from your monthly income will then have a lesser effect.

At this level, the vital need to save from your annual salary or business income will be greatly reduced, but should be continued nevertheless. Positive habits reinforces other positive habits and seeing regular positive cash flows coming in, helps psychologically.

The best you can do for your newborn child

Assume that you save $2,000 each year for your newborn child, and you continue saving for 10 years in a row the same amount (Total cash contributions $20,000). You would then stop contributing cash and let only the power of compounding take over at 15% p.a. (Figure 8-1). The results are astonishing. Upon your child's 18th birthday, you could present a cash gift of about $124,000. That would be an enormous amount for anyone to receive out-of-the-blue, regardless of education or career choice.

Figure 8-1

Family Investment Plan @ 15%			
Year	Yearly contribution	Interest Income	15%
1	2,000		2,000
2	2,000	300	4,300
3	2,000	645	6,945
4	2,000	1,042	9,987
5	2,000	1,498	13,485
6	2,000	2,023	17,507
7	2,000	2,626	22,134
8	2,000	3,320	27,454
9	2,000	4,118	33,572
10	2,000	5,036	40,607
11		6,091	46,699
12	Total 20,000	7,005	53,703
13		8,056	61,759
14		9,264	71,023
15		10,653	81,676
16		12,251	93,927
17		14,089	108,017
18		16,202	124,219
19		18,633	142,852
20		21,428	164,280
21		24,642	188,922
22		28,338	217,260
23		32,589	249,849
24		37,477	287,326
25		43,099	330,425
26		49,564	379,989
27		56,998	436,987
28		65,548	502,535
29		75,380	577,916
30		86,687	664,603
			Total Wealth Accumulation

Taking it a bit further at 15% annual compound rates, your child would have $660,000 on the 30th birthday, and a cool $2.7 million on the 40th birthday, provided you kept the money.

Of course, it is a hypothetical case and compounding money at 15% is extremely difficult. The message is, you should start saving as early as you can and for your children, too. If you compound your savings accordingly by being an 80/20 Investor, even small amounts of annual savings contributions a year have a huge impact on you or your family's future wealth.

Protect you Cash Portfolio

Make sure your cash is protected by either diversifying your cash among different banks and currencies, or by holding short-term government securities. Most importantly, your cash should be readily available without any penalty when the time comes and you want to withdraw. We will discuss more about Portfolio Management in Chapter 12.

The purpose of this cash portfolio is solely for building a long-term capital base for investment purposes. Under no circumstance should this portfolio be touched other than for investment purposes, outstanding business opportunities, or most dire personal emergencies such as accidents or illnesses. Let me clarify this: it's not a savings portfolio for your next consumer purchase, wedding ceremony, or vacation. That would be a secondary savings account called a consumption account.

A case for cash

You will hear many advisors and even highly respected investors making a case to be fully invested at all times and keep cash at a minimum. You will hear arguments about inflation cost or opportunity cost. You will hear arguments claiming that you can't time the market, it is never the right time to invest, so the right time is today. You will hear that cash is a dead asset that does not make you any money.

Ignore them! Nobody has to tell you that cash is an asset class with little or no returns, especially in a zero interest rate environment, and nobody should be telling you when to invest it. Cash has enormous advantages, such as being liquid when unique opportunities show up. It is the optionality of cash that is so highly appreciated by 80/20 investors. It's proven over and over again that holding cash or near cash safe securities from savings is an excellent default asset that has built the bases for great fortunes and wealth for individuals and whole countries alike. Always remember, 80/20 Investors intend to invest their cash, too, but on their own terms.

Savings is great, but ...

Japan's culturally entrenched attention to detail and organization is breathtaking and fascinating. Its society has unique cultural habits, such as their religious views or lack thereof, a strong sense of collectivism, and, by many accounts, an aversion to risk. This hasn't always been the case.

In the collapse of Japan's bubble economy in the early 1990s, a country generally known for its diligent savings ethics, was severely burned in mindless speculations, manipulations, and herd thinking. After these disastrous experiences, the Japanese middle class have tended to keep their savings in cash – literally in cash under their pillows or safely hidden in their small houses.

There is a wonderful quote by Mark Twain that describes the sentiment of the typical Japanese middle class: "A cat who sits on a hot stove will never sit on a hot stove again. But he won't sit on a cold stove, either." [58]

However, the wealthy Japanese elite continued investing, while still accumulating cash from their day-to-day businesses, even though they too experienced dramatic losses after the bubble economy era. What they understood is that, as investors who had healthy savings accounts and capital to continue investing, it is normal to experience losses from time to time, but it isn't the end of the world. They knew that investing over the long-term, if cleverly done, would more than compensate for the occasional losses along the way.

Saving is a great way to start building wealth. With adequate compound interest rates, you could see your money grow by itself. However, due to zero interest rates, you are forced to look for alternatives. The obvious solution is returns from investment operations. This will be discussed in the following chapters.

Action summary

- Convert your time into money through work and start saving early.
- Get a job you enjoy doing, that provides you with a decent living, and that allows you to save. Expensive degrees for high paying jobs are not necessary to have a better work-life balance and aspire to gain financial freedom.
- Always have a cash engine in place that brings in new cash each month, and that supports you even into retirement.
- Pay yourself first, even if you have high interest loans. Save between 3% and 10%, or more if you can afford to do so.
- Trick yourself into saving money by budgeting in advance and by finding cheaper goods – save the cash difference.
- Ask yourself whether you really need your next purchase. A penny saved is a penny earned, especially with the effect of compounding on your side as a powerful partner.
- Protect your cash and invest in short-term securities such as CDs (certificate of deposit).

By transforming your time into money through work and a disciplined savings plan, you will begin a powerful process. You will be on your way to financial freedom.

At the beginning, there is no other way than to work and save. But you have seen that it doesn't have to be for all your life, and it doesn't have to be large savings contributions. On the contrary, you have seen that the initial contributions from your actual work will dwarf the contribution from future investments at appropriate compound returns.

In the following chapters, you will focus on investment decision making and finding ways to generate adequate investment returns.

CHAPTER 9:
Make smarter decisions

"Often the difference between a successful person and a failure is not one's better abilities or ideas, but the courage that one has to bet on one's ideas, to take a calculated risk—and to act."

—ANDRÉ MALRAUX, FRENCH HISTORIAN

In the previous chapter, you learned that saving the 80/20 way is simple, and lays the foundation for your path to financial freedom. However, the issue of regular, stable, and, hopefully, high compound returns remains to be considered.

Compounding your cash with the simple interest rates of 10% is a thing of the past. You are now presented with a classic investor's dilemma: How do you achieve sufficient returns while minimizing risk?

It starts with the right mindset. Developing the proper mindset will influence all your decisions in investing.

The wrong mindset

Most people are overly fixated on specific numbers they need reach to be able to retire in comfort or to be able to stop working early. That leads them to mental shortcuts, which usually leads to unnecessary risks taken in the hopes of realizing their perfectly calculated retirement plan early. Simply put, they feel pressured.

From interviews with Mr. Standingback, I noticed how fixated he was on achieving early retirement, even though he didn't mind his day job. He was actually one of the best in his field, but the idea of early retirement was so strong that everything else in his life became secondary.

It was a positive force behind his saving efforts and willingness to take risks, but in the end, his fear of losing his hard-earned cash in face of terrible book losses made him panic. Twice. Later on, his fear of seeing prices drop also kept him away from investing when prices became so low that everybody else could recognize it. He had the wrong mindset, always standing-back from the action instead of waiting it out, and it resulted in him making disastrous decisions.

The right mindset

Be aware that you can't control the outcome of your investment returns; you can only control your actions. Instead of focusing on artificial target returns, focus on making better and smarter decisions.

All the 80/20 Investors you have read about had the right mindset. The mindset of a person who understands that financial markets are just a tool in the concept of wealth creation. A person who understands risk, the power of compounding, and most importantly, human nature is an 80/20 Investor. Mr. Womack didn't feel pressured to achieve stable monthly returns or even annual returns. He wasn't fixated on how to reach retirementment the fastest or most stable way. All he did was obey the seasons and go along his own business. He knew he had all the money he needed coming in, and making a few additional bucks on the mistakes of other market participants was "extra." He invested like a person who really wasn't dependent on making money in the stock market. He had the right mindset.

All 80/20 Investors understand that those with the wrong mindset (which is the majority of market participants) make mistakes in a predictable fashion, as the sun shines after rain and the night follows the day. The 80/20 Investor just has to wait to take advantage of this by making superior decisions.

The decision making process

Investing entails risk, and risk means that you could lose money occasionally for reasons that are beyond your control. However, you can make sure to reduce the possibility of errors by controlling your decision making process. Many investors commit errors, that could have been avoided with ease. These are known as "unforced errors." When reducing the rate of unforced errors, profitable investments will more than compensate for the occasional loss.

For 80/20 Investors, the entire process of making investment decisions is linked to risk management and avoidance of loss. As previously mentioned, overpayment risk (paying more for something that is worth way less) is a main focus for 80/20 Investors. It is in the very top 20% of most valuable tasks, right after cash management. Managing overpayment risk is vital, because any buying decision will set the stage for the rest of your investment journey. It will have a major impact on your investment performance, how relaxed you feel, and how well you sleep at night while holding your investments.

From here on, everything you do in **Step 3** is aimed at reducing overpayment risk and eliminating unnecessary errors through the reduction of your workload and any unnecessary complications, so that you always know what you are actually investing in.

Checklists - a simple concept

If you look back at the 80/20 Investors, you can see their decision making process was the pure essence of simplicity. What for an outsider seems like a spur of the moment decision, was for them an operation based on years of training, experience, and logical thinking.

We saw that all of them followed a kind of template, as their investments seemed to follow a pattern – starting from what they bought and when they bought it.

They all seemed to be using some sort of a mental checklist.

If this is true, you should be using checklists, too. Ideally these should be in written form, and handy for future reference. I came upon checklists for investing when I read Mohnish Pabrai's annual investor's transcripts[45]. He postulated that investors would gain great benefits if they used their own checklists, similar to those pilots and surgeons have been using for decades with great success.

The history and origin of the Aviation Checklist is a phenomenal story in itself. It's a story about how a simple concept, yet so powerful, could change the course of an entire industry that allowed it to be the safest transportation form we have to date. These are the tools for all 80/20 Investors.

On October 30th, 1935, the U.S. Army Air Corps held a flight competition for airplane manufacturers to decide on their next-generation long-range bomber. From the beginning, it was clear that Boeing Corporation's model 299 would win without much thought. Boeing's plane could carry five times as many bombs as the Army had requested; it could fly faster than previous bombers, and almost twice as far.

On that fateful day, the majestic silver aircraft took off, but it never saw the hangar of its airport again. The plane crashed after a standard test maneuver. Two of the five crew members died, including the pilot, Major Ployer P. Hill, a veteran in the industry and known for his excellent skills and many flight hours of experience.

What went wrong? An investigation revealed that nothing mechanical had gone wrong. The crash had been due to "pilot error," the report said. Substantially more complex than previous aircrafts due to its four engines than the usual two and the introduction of the latest aeronautic technology, it required the pilot to constantly go through each sequence in a specific order without intermission or breaks for rechecks. Major Hill had simply forgotten one step in a vital procedure of controlling the plane, while his attention was on a special flight sequence.

The test accident almost bankrupted Boeing, as it was deemed too complicated for one man to fly and not suitable for the army.

Nevertheless, some pilots at the air corps and a group of test pilots were convinced that the machine was flyable. They came up with an ingeniously simple approach: they created a pilot's checklist, with step-by-step checks for takeoff, flight, landing, and taxiing.

Everyone involved understood that this new plane had enormous potential, but it was just too difficult to be flown by memory alone, even for an outstanding pilot such as Major Hill. With the checklist in hand, the pilots went on to fly the Model 299 a total of 18 million miles without one accident. The Army ultimately ordered almost thirteen thousand of the aircraft, which it renamed the B17, also known as the "Flying Fortress." It would not only contribute to winning World War II, but thanks to the introduction of checklists, it would also contribute to the safety of an entire, rapidly growing industry.

Why checklists work

Checklists work because humans tend to overestimate their own capabilities in decision making, especially when we are under pressure or acting on emotions, such as fear or greed. We take mental shortcuts, simply ignoring important details, and do what Pabrai calls "mix[ing] ... rationality and emotions." [46] A mental, or better yet, a written, checklist forces you to go back and check all important aspects of each investment decision in a logical and rational sequence. It reduces errors of omission arising from mental shortcuts, and it can reduce any kind of emotional turmoil you might not be consciously aware of.

Remember, though, that 80/20 Investors never need to face a high-pressure situation like those encountered by pilots, surgeons, or even traders. Always take your time to go through your own carefully developed checklist.

What should be on checklists

The checklists that 80/20 Investors use vary, as they are based on personal experience or preference. However, the core of all checklists is the same and can be derived from the previous 80/20 Investors' examples:

Checklist

- Is cash management in place?
- Is it a no-brainer? Why?:
    - Is it in my circle of competence?
    - Does it contain a large margin of safety?
    - Calculate the maximum downside - overpayment risk?
- Can I say "no" to this idea?
- Do I obey the seasons for investing as Mr. Womack always observed?
- Can I commit a large portion of my cash reserves without having sleepless nights?
- Is my no-brainer opportunity in one of the *magic categories* that give me a competitive advantage?

Portfolio Management:
- Is sufficient diversification in place?
- Apply a step-in and step-out plan for buying and selling
- Check for emotional influences

Let's go through all the items one by one.

Cash management in place

We have already seen how important cash management is for 80/20 Investors. It provides you with the liquidity to buy investment opportunities where others might be forced to sell. It gives you a decisive psychological advantage. Trust me -- when everybody seems to be running for the exit, it can cause enormous subconscious self-doubt.

Knowing that more cash is coming in with each month, and knowing you have a portfolio of other great assets in place gives you the self-assurance you need, which will enable you to buy more of the same in case prices drop further.

No-brainer investments

Modern markets are efficient, but they do have their absurd moments from time to time, offering what I sometimes call "super bargains." You want these super bargains for the simple reason that they reduce risk and maximize returns. In the investment community, they are referred to as "no-brainers." No-brainers help simplify your decision-making and they reduce the risk of overpaying for an asset.

Charlie Munger, who made the expression "no-brainer" popular among investors, acknowledged that Berkshire Hathaway's enormous fortunes were based on "waiting for the no-brainers."

A no-brainer, according to Charles Munger, is an investment opportunity so obvious that you will make money. Once you have recognized a base investment case and its determining factors, "no-brainers" should present themselves without the use of over-complicated financial spreadsheets and calculations. One example would be Buffett's and Munger's purchase of Coca Cola shares in 1988 that became attractively priced after the 1987 stock market crash.

For neither Charlie Munger nor Warren Buffett has there been a need to be hyperactive or to invest in mediocre ideas just because cash was available. Their performance has been very successful by following a simple no-brainer strategy. Besides, their enormous asset size also doesn't allow them to invest in anything less than large, but very profitable and safe, investments.

A lot of value investors talk of valuation models such as discounted cash flows, and even Buffett mentions them occasionally, but Charlie Munger has this to say: "Warren often talks about these discounted cash flows, but I've never seen him do one." [46]

As long as you don't buy single securities of complex businesses, you don't need to do any classic valuation works with Excel spreadsheets or intricate computer software. The assumptions required in creating these spreadsheets or valuation software tempt you to use unrealistic future cash flow or interest rate predictions. According to Munger: "People calculate too much and think too little."

Even if you bought single securities, by focusing only on "no-brainers," the need for complex calculations is very limited, as the undervaluation or the cheapness of an investment idea should be so obvious you could do very simple calculations in your head. Mr. Womack, the farmer, just had a simple piece of paper where he jotted down his holdings and key numbers.

Privileging this type of intuitive work rather than concrete formulas might not be enough for the number crunchers and technical-biased investors, but it's enough for the 80/20 Investor.

Let me give you an example from the real world. If you were offered a new 50-inch TV on "Black Friday" for 90% off, there is no way you could ever lose on this deal. In the worst case, you would sell the TV for a nice profit at the nearest pawnshop. These super bargains are extremely rare. Fortunately, in the world of investing, these types of opportunities happen like clockwork, if you know where to look.

The determining factors for identifying no-brainers is that competence that leads to confidence, and confidence will distinguish an 80/20 Investor from the crowd, many of whom are too afraid to pull the trigger.

Circle of competence

"The only successful way to invest is to know what you are investing in, and to know it cold. If you do not know about an apple orchard in Washington, do not get into the apple business."

—Jim Rogers

The eminent economist, John Maynard Keynes wrote a letter to a business associate, F. C. Scott, on August 15, 1934 that referred to the power of having an area of expertise that supports the investment decision process, and improves its likelihood of being financially successful: "As time goes on, I get more and more convinced that the right method in investment is to put fairly large sums into enterprises which one thinks one knows something about and in the management of which one thoroughly believes. It is a mistake to think that one limits one's risk by spreading too much between enterprises about which one knows little and has no reason for special confidence.... One's knowledge and experience are definitely limited and there are seldom more than two or three enterprises at any given time in which I personally feel myself entitled to put full confidence."

Keynes managed the endowment of King's College, Cambridge from 1921 until his death in 1946 while working on his world changing publications. He outperformed the leading British equity index by an average of 8% [47] a year for over a quarter century, with the actively managed part of the endowment. It is rumored that he managed it from the safety of his bed each morning for 30 minutes, reading mainly newspapers and studying annual reports.

All 80/20 Investors are experts in their own area of interest or professional background, or what some value investors call a "circle of competence." This term refers to a field of industry or commerce one feels comfortable in and has either studied out of interest or has been involved in through his or her employment . Not only are 80/20 Investors experts in their respective circles of competence, they are also experts in valuation within this area.

They can distinguish between something valuable or a dud and can quickly assess the price they would be willing to pay for it. They only buy when they find something that represents extraordinary value to them, which is determined by cash flows or money inflows.

In a personal conversation, Mr. Standingback told me that he knew that Apple was profitable - it was all in the newspapers. After the NEXT deal in 1997, Steve Jobs started to restructure the company, and his efforts came to fruition with the launch of the iMac G3 in early 1999, along with its followup products. Mr. Standingback was also sure that Apple would grow -- all his co-workers and people in similar creative industries loved Apple's products -- it was just cool to have one. And even though he was not a valuation expert, he intuitively knew that this was just the beginning and more good things would come of Apple and Steve Jobs. He was assured that the price he bought Apple shares for in late 1998 were reasonable given their potential. He invested about $10,000 of his cash savings, which was most of his cash reserves, but only a minor part of his entire net wealth at that time. He had a stable job and cash left for sleeping comfortably at night. If only he had the confidence in his investment and competence to stay the course back then. I might not be using his story as a cautionary tale today.

Confidence - the gold example

The circle of competence is not an exact science, but more of an art. It is a helpful tool that will determine how comfortable you are with each investment you keep for a longer period of time; especially at times when the market prices seem to go sideways, slightly down, or even worse, crash to levels without any reason or logical explanation.

Let's assume your financial advisor recommended you buy gold at around $1,400 in late 2010 because it had been rising consistently, and it was touted as a protection against inflation and disaster -- a very popular scenario in 2010. Besides, it looked cool in your asset allocation pie chart. You are convinced and decided to buy 5 to 10% of your entire portfolio to invest in gold certificates or gold index funds. In the first couple of months, everything went according to plan - gold reached new record highs at over $1,900. But then somehow, gold lost its touch, going down month after month. Five long years later, as of December 2015, the price of gold is $1,070. If you had kept gold until this point, you must have gone through a very challenging time as an investor. You are now presented with a classic dilemma: to keep on holding it and risk further book losses; or to sell, realize a loss of 25%, and risk missing a strong recovery.

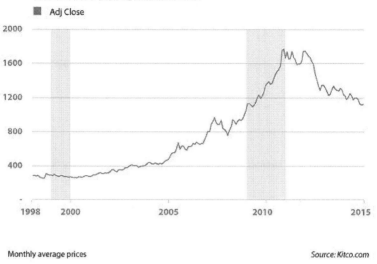

Gold Price ($/oz) since 1999

■ Adj Close

Monthly average prices   Source: Kitco.com

Gold is a great asset class with an impressive history worth studying, but like any other asset class, it obeys the laws of supply and demand, hence the price fluctuations. It, too, follows the same seasons Mr. Womacks described. There is time to buy gold and there is time to stay away from it, or even sell it. In the case above, there was neither strong confidence to buy gold, nor a real understanding of this uniquely challenging asset. In the end, you would have ignored the risk of overpayment, because it was bought for the wrong reasons and with a lack of understanding.

On the other hand, many gold experts who are physical gold buyers are very happy with keeping their physical gold for years or even forever. They don't mind the gold charts or overpayment risks. Their love for physical gold, the feeling of holding it in their hands, the strong belief that gold can help against inflation or economic and social disaster, represent all the value they need to buy and keep gold for many years in their vaults. It might never become the economic success they anticipate, but their love of holding it is more than enough compensation.

How to establish your own circle of competence?

Establishing your own circle of competence is easy. You start with your own profession or passion, and develop a strong core competence through continuous studies and gained experiences. Add to this the skill of assessing basic profitability and you are on your way to becoming an expert in assessing opportunities that will lead you to finding no-brainers.

An alternative way, or what I call a hybrid way, to building competence in an area of interest is to use a similar approach that was used by Mr. Standingback in his initial Apple investment. He was not working for Apple directly, nor was he involved in any technical developments, but he used its product in his daily work life. Follow and study companies that you come across due to your work or life passions, and that you admire for their products and services. They should have certain key economic characteristics, such as high profitability, simple business models, capable management and growth potential. Choose businesses that experience strong tailwinds rather than headwinds. Investing in a company that sells baby clothes in Japan might be an uphill struggle, but a company selling enterprise cloud software to technically inclined startups might be less of a challenge.

In each generation and geographic area, you can see trends emerging that support specific industries and companies rather than obstructing it. For Betty and her Gilded Age, it was real estate and railroad companies; for Getty it was oil; and, for Warren Buffett companies with strong brands profiting from globalization. Work on your circle of competence with zeal and enthusiasm, and you might be able to contradict Malcolm Gladwell's 10,000 hour rule. [48]

Margin of Safety

No-brainer opportunities are so obvious that you can't lose money. A core principle behind this concept is what value investors refer to as a "margin of safety," a concept first introduced by Benjamin Graham.

The original definition of margin of safety is essentially the gap between price and value. Perceived value by an investor can be made up by adding all tangible assets at market price, plus any intangible assets such as licences, brand value, and, most important of all, anticipated growth value. Growth, like anything else, can be priced by investors and is therefore part of valuing an investment. However, measuring growth potential is a very subjective field, because you are dealing with future forecasts, which are by definition uncertain. Consequently, pricing and forecasting growth requires a very strong circle of competence in order to gain confidence in growth valuations. The theories of valuations and the concept of margin of safety will play a more important role in single company investments, which will be a subject in my second book for advanced, active investors.

The wider the gap between market price and perceived value, the greater the safety level, and the more obvious the opportunity or no-brainer opportunity will become. Graham also explains that the margin of safety is important because it can absorb mistakes in assessing the value of an investment opportunity or, more specifically, the fair value of a business investment.

In more modern interpretations, a margin of safety not only constitutes the price differential between the perceived value and market price, but any additional safety that could support the valuation of an investment. For example, with additional dividend payments, the possibility of a government intervention in a strategic industry, such as banks, oil, or arms production can add to a safety margin. In the case of an index fund, the government or central bank itself could symbolize a certain margin of safety, with its economic rescue packages or quantitative easing policies.

In private investments, such as investing in business ventures or private real estate deals, you could constitute your own margin of safety by bringing your financial resources and expertise to the game. Just remember that no-brainer investments usually have a very wide margin of safety.

Calculate your maximum downside in advance

All 80/20 Investors should always evaluate the downside first before looking at the upside in order to honor the primary rule of investing: "never lose money." While calculating the downside, you will also be able to assess any overpayment risk. This is what Robert Rubin, former Secretary of the Treasury during the Clinton administration and former co-chairman of Goldman Sachs, called a "Probabilistic Approach" to decision making. As he postulates on the subject of decision making, "nothing is certain!" [49] According to him, a probabilistic approach helps you assess the pros and cons of an issue through a "highly conscious process".

"I imagine the mind as a virtual legal pad, with the factors involved in a decision gathered, weighted and totaled up" - "Sound decisions are based on identifying relevant variables and attaching probabilities to each of them. This is an analytic process but also involves subjective judgments. The ultimate decision then reflects all of this input, but also instinct, experience, and feelings." [51]

Try to calculate your maximum loss in a simple probability tree. The downside should never be more than the amount invested -- that is your default position. Avoid any kind of financial leverage, i.e., borrowing money to finance your investments. Passive 80/20 Investors should especially refrain from using financial leverage.

Let me give you an example. If you bought a single country index fund, your total loss could never be 100% as that would mean that all leading companies of that country had all gone bankrupt at the same time. From experience, extreme bubbles tend to represent a maximum loss of 90%. The crash of 1929 and the ensuing collapse of economic activity caused the Dow Jones Industrial Index to drop nearly 90% from its peak during the so-called Roaring Twenties. By July 8, 1932, the Dow closed the day at 41.22 coming down from over 400 in 1928. The extreme losses you would experience in such circumstance are very rare. You would only encounter them if you had bought at the very peak and held on until the very bottom.

For example, if you had bought Japan's Nikkei 225 in December 1989 at around 38,000 and sold in February 2009 at around 7,300 you would have lost about 80% of your value over a period of 20 years, not including any dividend payments, opportunity cost, or inflation/deflation adjustments.

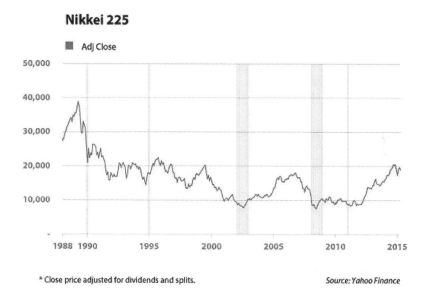

Nikkei 225

■ Adj Close

* Close price adjusted for dividends and splits.   *Source: Yahoo Finance*

If you bought an index fund, much more diversification would not be necessary, as indices are already well-diversified. If you bought a single company, which applies excessive financial leverage, the risk of losses is very real, and you could lose your entire investment. The same counts for any startup commitment or any new business endeavor you might want to support financially. Compared to investments in index funds, more, but efficient, diversification would be prudent.

Calculating the downside first is a strong test of whether you would be psychologically prepared for quoted prices to turn against your interests. You will feel very different when your investment shows as a fat, red number in the downturn column. If you can live with red numbers for an extended period of time, it would demonstrate your confidence and faith in your investment. It would indicate whether you have done your homework. Charlie Munger had this confidence in 1973 and 1974, knowing very well that his portfolio represented outstanding no-brainer ideas at ridiculous prices, and so did Buffett. He was right -- his portfolio recovered dramatically in 1975.

Can I just say "No"?

One of the most valuable skills in investing is the ability to say "no." All great investors I know had this skill – Nathan Mayer Rothschild, Henry Singleton, and Benjamin Graham had it, and, most certainly, Warren Buffett and Charlie Munger have it, too. As mentioned before, nobody should ever be able to force you into a decision you will later regret -- don't let your power to decide be taken away by people who pretend to know better than you. Don't let yourself be pushed into a decision you feel uncomfortable with, doesn't make sense to you, or is just not in your circle of competence. Using your own checklist will help you enforce your own "no" policy.

There are countless counterarguments to this policy. Some might say that inflation will eat your saved capital away, or that you might miss a lot of opportunities. That might all be true, but you will also avoid a lot of failures and substantial losses. For the purpose of wealth creation, the ability to say "no" is the most valuable skill to have. Practice the discipline of reserving the right to say "no," and see your wealth increase.

Is it the right season?

Mr. Womack argued that you can't invest in stocks, bonds, or real estate at just any point of time, just as you can not plant seeds any time of the year. In any investment category, there is a season for buying and there is season for selling.

There is no exception.

For example, if you have seen markets boom for several years in a row and there is an excess of liquidity in the market driven by easy money and artificial demand, you should be very careful with your buying operations and instead consider using the abundance of liquidity for selling some of your positions.

In history, a few clever investors have always made use of what I call "liquidity clouds". Liquidity moves like clouds with seasons. These investors sold positions when there was plenty of liquidity in the markets, and always bought when the liquidity dried up dramatically and no buyers were found anywhere else. When there is a sudden, unexpected dry season, you will see hordes of desperate market participants rush for the last remaining water hole. Inevitably, this highly sought after pool is controlled by 80/20 Investors. Obey the seasons!

Large positions - large impact

Ask yourself if you are willing to commit most of your saved cash. If you can't invest a substantial amount of money in one investment, because you feel uncomfortable and you have no confidence, you should not invest. But if you have identified a rare no-brainer opportunity, you have calculated your maximum downside, and done your homework, it is time to commit, and commit in force. It's not enough to just dip your toes into a position and not follow up. This is what you have been saving and preparing yourself for a long time.

From the very beginning, you need to commit yourself to deploy a large portion, or even most of the cash you have accumulated over months and years. These are the rare opportunities that make the performance differences that reverberate for many years to come. These investments will be your compound return powerhouses that will blow away any professional investor who dares to lecture or criticize you. Take no prisoners and commit your money!

Action summary

The last remaining points on the checklist list will have their own chapters.

Let me summarize what we have discussed so far on the matter of checklists and making better investment decisions based on the 80/20 principle.

CHAPTER 10:
Where to look & what to buy

"Buy low, sell high"

—A FAMOUS INVESTING ADAGE

What should I buy and when should I buy? How much should I buy? These are the most common questions among individual and institutional investors.

Regarding these questions, Charlie Munger has this to say:

"A few major opportunities, clearly recognizable as such, will usually come to one who continuously searches and waits, with a curious mind that loves diagnosis involving multiple variables. And then all that is required is a willingness to bet heavily when the odds are extremely favorable, using resources available as a result of prudence and patience in the past." [50]

It's pure simplicity! To elaborate more on Munger's quote, I would like to show you two different sources of investment ideas, because, in the end, the secret to finding great opportunities is to search in the right places, and that differs from person to person.

There are only two approaches to finding investment opportunities. A work-intensive way and an easy way:

1. **Search** continuously in various markets and asset classes for promising investment leads and try to be early at the party. This approach is work intensive and risky at times!

2. **Wait** until someone or something offers a no-brainer opportunity - This approach is not work intensive and carries less investment risk.

I call it the Amazon vs. the Farming approach. Amazon always offers you plenty of ideas about how to spend your money. Using the Amazon approach, you just have to search for something you like. Whether or not the purchase makes sense or you really need it doesn't matter.

Most investors, whether private or professionals, follow this approach to investing. They have money and they want to invest it right away. Whether it is the right season is of less importance, because they feel confident to always find the right investment ideas whatever season it is. Wall Street fully supports their confidence.

The farming approach is different, as Mr. Womack explained. In farming, there is a strict season you have to obey to be able to sow and to be able to harvest. In between, there is nothing much you can do, however much you like to speed up the process. You just can't force it -- so why not relax and wait for the seasons to unfold.

Where the professional investor is obliged and under pressure to find investment opportunities on a daily basis using the first method, the enthusiast investor, or active individual investors, do this for the sheer love of the game. They search in different asset classes, industries, and even countries. With each new investment idea, they need to build up a knowledge base quickly in order to establish a circle of competence that gives them confidence for their investment decision. Their performance comes from getting in early, identifying new consumer habits, and noting business trends that promise growth, before the masses jump on an accelerating train.

This type of investing includes angel investing, venture capital, and growth investing. Needless to say, this requires time and financial resources, a very quick and analytical mind, and a higher appetite for risk.

For the 80/20 Investor, I strongly recommend the second approach. Adopting a more passive strategy has some clear advantages. You make less mistakes, save money in fees and resources, and are in a much stronger position to take advantage of opportunities. Besides, you will have plenty of time to do your day job, grow your own business, or just follow your other passions.

Category Nr. 1 - The Base Category

That still leaves you with some key questions. How does one find no-brainer opportunities? Where does one look for them?

According to the World Federation of Exchanges, at the end of 2013 there were over 5,000 companies listed in the U.S. alone. Add to this European and Japanese stocks and you have a possible universe of over 10,000 listed companies that you could research and invest in. Don't forget all those mutual funds, hedge funds and exchanged traded funds investors could consider. At the end of 2012, there were 7,238 mutual funds available to investors, according to Morningstar.

You could start researching from "A", and never finish the list in your lifetime. Or, you could use one of those many filtering tools that screen through all databases according to your own set of parameters. This technique is a standard procedure of professional and amateur investors alike. With the dramatic increase in computer processing power, there has been every possible screening method processed under the sun. But I ask you: why would a rational investor venture out in areas and industries he knows nothing about, and has no knowledge advantage whatsoever, just because a computer program tells him to? The 80/20 way to finding investments targets is very different from the standard method used by professional investors.

Look at home

The most logical area to look for opportunities is within your own work environment, your own business expertise, or within your own interests, in the area that constitutes your chosen circle of competence.

In its purest form, the first and most logical investment that constitutes a no-brainer decision is to invest in yourself. That could mean an investment in education or a specific skill set that could boost your immediate earnings potential. This could be in specific equipment which could help you do your job better and more efficiently. Finally, consider investments in business networks. I never get tired of recommending that investors join active and first class networks that boost their personal value. My personal best investment in 2015 was joining the DC network, an international, high quality community of location independent entrepreneurs and investors. For me, this investment has already paid off many times over. Joining a relevant community based on your personal background could do the same for you.

Logically, investing in yourself first is an approach that requires a fraction of the time professional investors use for just searching and screening a universe of several asset classes, which can comprise thousands of companies.

Rather than searching for investments on which you have no prior experience or knowledge advantage, you decide right from the start what you can and want to invest in based on your own personal background and preferences. In its most basic form, you already decide in advance on a few investments to focus on and seldom deviate from.

For example, James Rothschild always wanted to buy Chateau Lafite, since he had a passion for great wine and the wine business. He instantly understood the value of Chateau Lafite. He waited a life-time for this opportunity, and finally he succeeded.

J. Paul Getty bought oil stocks in the crash of 1962, because that was his area of expertise. Before the crash, it was clear to him what he would invest in. Mr. Standingback noticed Mac computers in his own work environment and how popular, user-friendly, and stylish they were. Naturally, he always owned Macs and to this day he owns several.

If you were a software developer who knew a lot about cloud computing, you would instantly be familiar with software companies such as Salesforce.com. If you were working in food marketing, your would clearly be familiar with Nestle, Mondelēz International or Yum! Brands. The point here is that there would never be a need to screen thousands of companies in industries you don't know anything about and haven't even heard of.

Animal smell and a $20 million check

Consider the story of Jerry Yang, former CEO of Yahoo, and Masayoshi Son, the founder and CEO of Softbank and Yahoo Japan, and their early investment in Alibaba.

In 2005, under Yang's direction, Yahoo purchased a 40% stake in Alibaba for $1 billion. He knew the asset would be hugely valuable someday and he refused to sell Yahoo to Microsoft when Steve Ballmer tried to acquire his company in 2008, a decision which cost him his CEO job. His belief in Jack Ma, the founder of Alibaba, was unshakeable. "Once you meet an entrepreneur like Jack Ma, you just want to make sure you bet on him," he said. "It's not a hard decision." [51] In other words, it was a no-brainer decision for him.

That he was ousted from Yahoo was actually the best thing that could have happened to him. Yang founded his own company in an area he had a strong passion for, and that guaranteed his personal breathing space. "I wanted to be able to do things at my own pace," he said. "I wanted to make mistakes and nobody would care. People who observe me say I'm so much happier." Ironically, Yahoo has become a proxy for Alibaba and nothing more, and only Yang got a seat on Alibaba's board, nobody else from Yahoo did. [53]

The story of Masayoshi Son, an entrepreneur and shrewd investor, is even more impressive. His investment in Alibaba illustrates his thought process and decision making. His strength: he trusts his instincts, based on his expertise and experience collected over many years in the trenches.

Son recalls that when he first sat down with Jack Ma in 2000, "I had already met the chiefs of 20 internet businesses, but he was the only one who convinced me his company would achieve overwhelming growth." He further added, "the look in [Ma's] eye" and his "animal smell. It was the same when we invested in Yahoo, when they were still only five or six people." [53]. One might call this intuition or a sixth sense, but for Son this meeting gave him all the information necessary to make a decision.

After the meeting, Son instantly decided to invest $20 million in Alibaba, which was less than a year old and technically broke. For Son, it was an obvious no-brainer decision. That Son made such a substantial investment at a time when he himself suffered from the aftermath of the dotcom bubble is even more impressive. In late 2000s, his company, Softbank, lost 99% of its market cap from its peak valuations.

Son and Yang made a fortune on their early investment decision. In 2012, Yahoo sold a portion of its stake in Alibaba for $7.6 billion.[53] The company made an additional $9.4 billion in Alibaba's 2014 IPO. [54]

Son wasn't finished yet. He kept his 34.4% stake in Alibaba. It was worth $57.8 billion at the time of the Initial Public Offering (IPO) in 2014. He waited for almost 14 years to see the payout and he is still holding on to his shares. He doesn't need to sell. That is long-term investing at its finest, where one single decision can make all the difference and everything else pale in comparison.

The above story is not to demonstrate how the juggernauts of business are lucky to get the best deals before anybody else, but to demonstrate their mindset and thought process as successful investors who understand their trade.

Neither Yang nor Son ventured out in areas they knew nothing about, but sought out opportunities in their respective industries, within their circle of competence. Both understood the e-commerce business by heart and knew of the growth and potential profit China could offer them if they found the right person and the right investment opportunity. They found that person in Jack Ma and, ultimately, in Alibaba. Note that Son had already searched for some time and had several interviews with Chinese CEOs. What he had to do was obvious once he met Ma through Jerry Yang. He trusted his own gut feeling that he had built over many years with start-up, and specifically with internet related start-up companies. After all, he was the owner and manager of one of the most prominent internet start-up companies in Japan.

The confidence they both had in their investment decision was astonishing. This kind of confidence can only be the result of knowing what they were doing. Losing on this investment would not have been the end of the world either--however painful it would have been for their egos. Besides, they both had free cash flow coming in from their existing business operations which could have financed new investments.

The bigger picture for Son was to develop his Softbank business in Japan, his core cash generator that includes Yahoo Japan, a broadband, and now a US telecommunication business. I am certain that when he prepared to take over Vodafone Japan from Vodafone Plc. in 2006, or when he acquired Sprint Nextel in 2012, Alibaba was one of the last things on his mind.

Some readers today might say, "well, it is obvious to invest in China and Alibaba." Yes, in hindsight it might have been, but investing in China in 2000 or even 2005 wasn't that obvious for the majority of us. Only a person with a strong circle of competence and the resulting insight could have made a similarly bold decision.

No-brainers are for everyone

No-brainer opportunities don't happen only to the business leaders of Fortune 500 businesses, as in the cases we just discussed. They happen all around you, in your own personal professions or in your own businesses.

Consider the story of Brendan Tully, founder and principal consultant at The Search Engine Shop, an Australian based web consultancy that specializes in internet marketing and related consulting services.

Tully always had a knack for seeing opportunity where others couldn't. A true entrepreneur, he developed several companies from scratch with enormous success, but also with a fair share of failures and mistakes. Nevertheless, what he understood early on was that life would offer opportunities to the person who is willing to accept challenges and who is able to take action.

Such an opportunity came along in 2011. When, while talking to his existing clients for his SEO and web marketing business, he constantly heard complaints about how bad and unreliable their hosting services were, an issue he was himself familiar with.

What his clients described was one of the vital IT issues every internet business eventually suffers from. Clients would break something on their internet platform, and their hosting would go down. Many times it would go down even without breaking anything and often for a couple of days at a time. Consequently, their SEO and Ads stopped working. These outages, resulted in large revenue losses for Tully's clients in addition to the storm of complaints they received from their own clients.

For anybody in business, especially internet business, this is the worst possible scenario—disgruntled clients leave and money stops flowing. For some reason, people kept calling Tully for help, even though it obviously wasn't his company's responsibility, but that of the existing hosting services.

It was under these circumstances that something clicked for Tully. It was not only a business opportunity, but it was such an outstanding and obvious opportunity, that he asked himself why he hadn't seen it earlier. [55] He made a quick back-of-the-envelope calculation and realized what anyone should have seen: this was a no-brainer decision. He calculated that his initial investment would be less than $2,000 and his breakeven point could be achieved with less than three customers, his first customer being his own company.

Within a couple of months, he had signed up four more clients, quicker than he expected. Only four years later, he has a customer base of 200, a six figure business, and a growth trajectory that seems to be exponential.

By nearly sheer coincidence, he created a new business from scratch, with recurring profits, growth potential, and high profit margins that also worked as a platform for cross selling his other existing products and services.

When asked how he recognized this opportunity and how he made the crucial decision so quickly, he answered that it was just so obvious and the initial risk was minimal – he felt he couldn't lose. [57]

Tully has a deep background in IT, IT infrastructure, SEO, and online marketing. At that time, in 2011, Tully already ran an IT company with a staff of 20 and hundreds of clients for more than 8 years. He and his team understood the underlying technology of how hosting worked for himself and his clients. It was within his circle of competence that he was able to recognize this opportunity, and, being an entrepreneur, he knew he had to take action.

For Tully, it was a clear no-brainer to spend the couple of thousands that eventually became one of his most profitable businesses.

Action summary

Your work environment, your own business, or even your personal hobbies should be the main source for your best investment opportunities. You have an instant information and experience advantage. Scrutinize your own field of expertise or passion and develop an eye for no-brainer opportunities instead of mindlessly copying TV celebrities or your favorite investment manager you have been following. Especially as an owner and manager of a business, you will have all the data and information to make the best assessment of each opportunity that presents itself to your business. If you cannot distinguish between a great investment opportunity and a mediocre one within your own business field, you might have trouble finding one somewhere else.

Having said that, we cannot all be like Son, Yang, or Tully either. Quite frankly, I couldn't have made all those decisions, even if they had dipped my face into a stack of cash and used all sorts of mind tricks to convince me. I still would have stared at them with a Homer Simpson-like stare, for the simple reason that I don't understand anything about their industries and thus have no confidence to make a well reasoned decision, or the confidence to hold such an investment in times of declining markets. For me, it would have never been a "no-brainer" idea -- obviously it was for them. So are there more categories where individual investors with normal day jobs could apply the 80/20 way to finding no-brainer investment ideas? Yes, there are, and they will be discussed in the the next chapter.

CHAPTER 11:
Use The Magic Categories

"In a crisis, be aware of the danger - but recognize the opportunity."

—JOHN F. KENNEDY, 35TH U.S. PRESIDENT

On March 11, 2003, Japan's largest banks, dragged down by years of mismanagement and non-performing loans (NPL), were technically all bankrupt. At that time, I was a young equity analyst trainee at a German securities company in Tokyo. On that fateful day, as part of my training program, I was sitting next to a veteran equities sales trader watching his four trading monitors. I had read all the books on cool traders, the trading culture that was sometimes celebrated, and, of course, the history those in finance had made. I was able to quote from Michael Lewis' *Liar's Poker* [56] in my sleep -- his book was genius for a young ambitious trainee, working in investment banking. I would have never thought that I myself would one day experience a similar scene as that was depicted in his book: when he describes the bizarre atmosphere on the trading floor during the crash of October 1987.

There I was, sitting next to that old timer veteran stock trader, a Japanese version of a "big swinging dick," watching with awe as the scenario was unfolding in front of us: the largest banks of the second largest economy in the world, Japan, were slipping into oblivion minute by minute-- -5%, -8%, -10%, and falling. The trader's monitor was completely covered in red. It felt like a scene from *Das Boot* (1981), when the captain can't stop his submarine from sinking into the abyss and everybody, covered in sweat, watches the depth gauge with mouths agape.

The Japanese bank stocks kept on going down, and dragged all other sectors with them. It was fascinating in a way, even though we both knew that a lot of pension funds, insurance companies, and hedge funds were losing billions of yen at that same moment. A full-blown panic swept over the Japanese equities market.

The rumors were that at least one of the three largest commercial banks would go bankrupt, similar to LTCB (Long Term Capital Bank) a couple of years before, causing a market shock that would reverberate around the world.

I remember clearly the head of equities at that time running up and down the corridors of the trading floor, frantically looking over the shoulder of his trading team, shakingly announcing his certainty, "I bet Mizuho Bank will go bankrupt -- I am sure of it -- trade accordingly. No way will the Japanese government initiate a bailout for that piece of junk." At that time, I wouldn't dare question his reasoning and conclusions. As he was head of equities and my boss, his salary was probably 10 times mine at that time. Actually, I flat out believed him -- after all, he had been in the markets for more than a decade, and his opinion seemed to be the general market consensus reflected in the continuously falling share prices.

Suddenly, I noticed the equities sales trader mumbling to himself, "Something is going on. Someone is buying my bank shares! Not much, but someone is buying!" We couldn't believe it. Who could be so suicidal to dare to buy bank shares at that moment? We were all sure that more disaster was in the making -- even bigger than the financial crisis following the 9/11 attacks.

The day ended with Japanese banks closing at almost limit low. It was brutal -- real carnage. Nervous and anxious clients called non-stop to find out the damage and to get some reassuring comfort from our sales traders. But we knew, and they knew themselves, that no comforting word could help them forget the billions of dollars they lost that day. The well-known Wall Street expression "when there is blood in the streets" became almost a reality for at least some bankers and investors. The Nikkei 225, the Japanese national stock market index, reached its new post-bubble low of 7,862, coming from a height of 38,915 at the end of December 1989.

Little did we know at the time, the mysterious buyer of our bank shares was a secretive investing group known as "Sovereign Global Holdings," which was founded by the New Zealand-based Chandler brothers, Richard and Christopher, to manage their family funds. When everybody else seemed to dump shares in a panic selling frenzy, they calmly and methodically executed their buying plan of mass purchasing Japanese bank shares.

They began secretly buying back in November 2002 with the cash reserves accumulated over years from their independently managed family fund, paying $570 million for a 5.1% stake in UFJ Holdings, which had posted a staggering loss of $9.3 billion in its latest year. The pair went on to buy more than 3% of Mizuho Financial Group, the bank my former boss declared bankrupt. All in all, they bought sizeable stakes in several other banks, such as Sumitomo Mitsui Banking Corp. and Mitsubishi Tokyo Financial Group (which merged with UFJ in January). Altogether, they spent about $1 billion on a diversified portfolio of near-dead Japanese banking shares. [57]

"The banks were priced for a total wipeout of equity holders," mentioned Sovereign's broker at Nikko Citigroup, John Nicholis. "We were advising our clients to stay away from the sector," he said. [57]

The Chandler brothers obviously ignored their banker's advice, as they had so many times before that. It was the right decision. After the banking share massacre that day, the Japanese government announced, in a nervously anticipated press conference, that it would provide emergency funds to the leading commercial banks and nationalize Rezona Bank, a mid-sized retail and commercial bank. The headlines the next day read: "As stocks fall, Japan moves to prop up banks." [58] The US government isn't the only one well versed in bailing out bankers.

Japan's economy recovered by the end of 2003 thanks, in part, to the Bank of Japan and the FED, which was then headed by Chairman Alan Greenspan, who was pumping massive amounts of liquidity into the U.S. economy. Within a couple of years, all banks eagerly returned the government's emergency loans with interest, trying to end their chapter of national shame. In 2006, the Nikkei 225 surged to 17,000, in a gain which represented more than 200%. The country's banks had recovered by then, forming the so-called three "Mega Banks."

And the Chandler brothers? Well, it is estimated that they made a killing of over $2 billion on an initial investment of $1 billion, representing an annualized return of about 44.2% (200% capital gains within 3 years). This represents an unbelievable head start of more than 8 years competing with investors who have 10% annual return expectations. It simply means, that the Chandler brothers could have retired from investing for almost 8 years and still enjoy the same annual investment returns as investors who most likely struggle to make 10% each year for 11 years in a row (200% at 10% annually compounded takes about 11 years). Making a few simple decisions, derived from years of experience and expertise in the field of banking and Japanese financial markets, they let their money work for them and it showed results. This is 80/20 Investing applied to perfection.

Figure 11.1

Chandler Brothers Portfolio			CAGR
Start	2002	$1 billion	
End	2006	$3 billion	32%

Target Annual Return			10%
No. Years	2002	1.0	
1	2003	1.1	
2	2004	1.2	
3	2005	1.3	
4	2006	1.5	CAGR 32%
5	2007	1.6	
6	2008	1.8	
7	2009	1.9	
8	2010	2.1	
9	2011	2.4	
10	2012	2.6	
11	2013	2.9	
12	2014	3.1	CAGR 10%

Compound Annual Growth Rate

Understanding the mechanics of 80/20 Investing, they couldn't help but take advantage of subsequent no-brainer ideas that came their way. Afterall, why should you retire from investing when you know how the game is played. One subsequent no-brainer opportunity came along only 3 years later. In May 2009, it became public that the Chandler Brothers again had built up massive concentrated positions in stocks. According to newspaper reports Richard Chandler had built a position worth $US430 million in a Russian bank, called Sberbank, shortly after the main Russian stock market index (RTS) passed its low in March 2009, due to the subprime crises in the US.

Both Chandler brothers were experts in Russian stocks and the Russian stock market, as they had invested there in years past. They revisited the market, but now with much more cash to invest, and the prices they got this time were pure no-brainer material.

The concentrated position in Sberbank Russia's leading bank represented 3% of their outstanding shares. That is an investment that became public due to regulation. Within only two months, Chandler's initial investment in Sberbank almost doubled. As Mark Twain said, "History doesn't repeat itself, but it does rhyme." [59] For the Chandlers, it rhymed beautifully. I am certain that they are preparing themselves for the next no-brainer situation that will surely come along their way probably sooner than later.

More magic categories

Aside from searching within your own profession and circle of competence (Category Nr. 1), as suggested in the previous chapter, there are four more areas that offer universal opportunities for any 80/20 Investor, regardless of their specific work background or expertise. These are areas that put maximum emphasis on the price that you have to pay to get value, with less reliance on expert knowledge and confidence about the inherent growth potential of a specific business opportunity.

The underlying principle behind these categories is to observe the seasons, as Mr. Womack so masterfully expressed. To see it from a different perspective, you let the market bring ideas to you rather than go chasing after hot investment tips.

Imagine you're the Godfather. Yes, the one from the movies, the one with the antique wooden desk in the dimly lit office which probably smells of tobacco. You're just like Brando. You examine your paperwork with one lazy sweep of your hand. You don't have meetings; you have audiences. If financial market is in desperate need of your help (your money), you will grant it. But at your prices and on your terms -- and to your benefit!

The following idea categories represent the 80/20 way to investing, because they help you to focus on the decision that will have the largest impact on your portfolio's performance. They will reduce your workload and simplify your decision making, while ensuring enormous performance results for your portfolio without the need for advanced technical or accounting knowledge. Mr. Womack, the pig farmer, most certainly didn't have an MBA or an advanced accounting degree. He didn't need to! All the 80/20 Investors I have introduced so far made use of one or more of the following four categories, and so should you.

All Magic Categories:

1)   Your personal Circle of Competence
2)   Global market crises
3)   Single country crises
4)   Individual industry crises or single asset class depression
5)   Single business/company crises

The four additional categories, even though great starting points for no-brainer ideas, require you to do your own analysis and homework, with the top one requiring the least and the bottom one requiring the most. The fifth category requires more specific business understanding and effort, but could be made of use by anybody who is willing to take more time and do more research.

Category Nr. 2 - Global stock market panics

Global crises are few and far between, which is good news for the general population. However, they do offer all 80/20 Investors some really outstanding investment opportunities, as long as you have a cash portfolio in place, and you are not forced to sell any of your existing holdings.

These types of crises have been studied extensively by academics and investment professionals alike. They occur over long time cycles of roughly 20 to 30 years and drag down entire economies around the world. They are powerful, and they can depress market prices for all asset classes to ridiculously low levels for extended periods. During these periods, there is simply no demand for these asset classes, and this causes prices to plummet for everything, including gold and real estate.

Probably the three largest panics we've had over the last 100 years were:

1929-1939 -- The Great Depression
1970s -- Global Energy Crises
2007-2009 -- Subprime Crises

We had many more crashes and panics in between, but these three stand out. Most of them derive from crises in the financial sector. Such crises include the recent subprime crises, sovereign debt or budgetary concerns, and also price level concerns among leading global economies, like the oil shock in the 70s. If you look closely and honestly at the current national debt situations of the U.S., Japan, or even France and Germany, combined with a detailed demographic analysis, you must make note of the pending debt crises that could derail global financial markets.

Let me explain. In order to manage these high debt levels, a permanent low interest rate environment is required. Maintaining such an environment is unrealistic and actually detrimental for long-term economic health. As in Japan, there will be more and more "zombie companies," which can only survive with low interest rates. By keeping interest rates low, national regulatory bodies stave off the natural cleansing process that market forces usually bring about at all cost. Any increase in rates would have dramatic consequences for these debt ridden companies, as well as their governments.

Add to this possibility of any kind of unanticipated disaster, such as a catastrophic terrorist attack on U.S. soil, or a major earthquake in Tokyo, and you have to realize that we haven't seen the last global financial crises of our lifetime.

Predicting world crises in terms of timing is impossible, even though you can usually see the writing on the wall way in advance when something is amiss in the financial system. I would advise you to follow interest rates in the US and Japan very closely. Any change upward will have a dramatic impact on global valuations, zombie companies, and on sovereign and corporate debt. Forecasting crises, however, is not the purpose of this book. We are more interested in the opportunities these events bring after they occur and unfold themselves completely.

Bottom prices

Now the biggest concern many investors typically have is not finding a bottom or being stuck for several years in investments that don't seem to move. When they read the headlines in the newspaper, it can freeze anyone, especially when there seems to be a never-ending stream of more bad news and more shocking revelations from experts and economists. For some, it feels like the end of the world is near. Many worry that prices will continue to go down; in fact, they do. However, these concerns are of no relevance for 80/20 Investors' long-term performance for the following reasons.

1. Their aim is not to time markets, but to buy great assets at great prices -- no-brainers. It is not their intention to buy at the lowest point and aim to sell at the top. That would defeat the purpose.

2. They have replenishing cash portfolios in a place where they can take the opportunity to buy more at better prices. They merely buy something great at even greater prices.

Mr. Womack, who didn't care for the old stock market wisdom-- "never send good money after bad"-- even added to his position when markets got cheaper. He was happy that he finally found a place for his cash, where it could be of use and worked for him.

Here you should appreciate the importance of having a functional cash management system in place your read about in Chapter 8, that distinguishes 80/20 Investors from other investors, especially the institutional ones. Mutual funds, hedge funds, and other institutional funds have to fight with redemptions in a panic and in a multi-year recession. It forces them to liquidate their positions even though their Fund Managers know for certain that these holdings will be profitable in the future.

Category Nr. 3 - Single country Panic

In August 1982, Mexico was the first of many Latin American countries to default on its sovereign debt. The Mexican economy contracted rapidly as many banks were struggling and many foreign investors were leaving the the country completely. It was a real economic crisis with the pesos, the local currency of Mexico, losing value rapidly and with many businesses going bankrupt. The following recession years were difficult for the country and its people.

During this time, a relatively unknown local businessman, who had patiently accumulated cash from his family business, started buying and investing heavily in Cigatam, a Mexican tobacco company, at what some experts called "fire sale" prices. He ended up controlling the company, and continued using his cash savings to buy Mexican assets at low prices. Very soon, he began using Cigatam's free cash flow to fund even more purchases. After all, who wants to give up smoking during a stressful recession?

He bought interests in chemicals, manufacturers, retail operations, food, and even financial service providers. In effect, he bought a basket of the finest companies of all Mexico--a premium version of Mexico's economy carefully chosen by quality and future potential. During this period, this unknown man laid the groundwork to becoming the richest man in the world, as ranked by *Forbes Magazine* in 2013. His name is Carlos Slim Helú.

Slim, in effect, made a huge investment on the future of his home country, betting that Mexico would survive the most severe recession to date. He bet that the entrepreneurial spirit of business owners would survive, recover, and regain strength with or without government support. Who could have made this kind of investment except a native of Mexico, a person who understood the ins and outs of his economy, the business community, and its leaders?

When Slim was interviewed, he was asked for the secret to his success. He said that his success stems from his admiration for his father Julian, who emigrated from Lebanon at age 14 and made his fortune investing in property in the 1910-17 Mexican revolution. He also said that he was inspired by American oil billionaire, J. Paul Getty. Slim learned of Getty's business acumen as a young boy and had gone on to mirror his money making skills. It pays to have the right role models in life. [60]

The ugly Cousin

The ugly cousins of a global crises are single country panics. In the last 20 years, I personally have experienced a handful of single country crises myself within and outside OECD countries (Organisation for Economic Co-operation and Development). There was the Asian Crisis in 1997, Russia in 1998, Argentina in 2002, Japan in 2003, and in recent years, Iceland, Ireland, Portugal, and Greece to name just a few prominent cases. The best opportunities are crises that occur in nations that previously had functional markets and a good record of upholding the law.

For the sake of minimizing risk, I would suggest focusing on OECD (Organisation for Economic Co-operation and Development) countries describing themselves as committed to democracy and the market economy. Rarely should you go outside this pool of countries unless you have advanced knowledge and expertise about the non-OECD nations in question.

Most national crises stem from banks or financial mismanagement by governments. Few occur due to natural catastrophes.

The Asian crises derived from political mismanagement of state finances, whereas Japan's 2003 collapse was a classic banking crisis -- an old legacy from the bubble years dragged along until the financial system couldn't take it any longer, and a bailout became necessary. Something similar happened to Iceland, Ireland, and Greece in the recent past. Again, index funds or a pool of the leading listed corporations should do the trick to participate in any recovery and return to normal economic circumstances.

National crises that originate through budgetary mismanagement or financial system failure are great opportunities to buy excellent local, or even world brand, companies at wonderful prices. Again, they are very easy to identify by just reading the newspaper headlines. One needn't be hasty with purchases, as these situations usually unfold over period of several months, sometimes years.

Country crises usually fall within most of an individual's circle of competence, especially when the country in question is your home country, as in Slim's case. But even if you venture abroad and do some research on brand companies you already know, you can buy a basket of them with confidence.

Building a portfolio with a national index fund or portfolio of assorted leading companies in the country is a good and safe way to build up a sizeable position for your investment portfolio. Add to the position when markets do get cheaper, but take the time to cover yourself with some background checks. It would also be prudent to take some cash off the table once your country index funds has more than doubled. Japan has always been the point in case. Fundamental and economic reasons would always dictate a more cautious approach to a country, such as Japan, that has to deal with massive demographic challenges and an ever increasing debt burden that hasn't been resolved yet.

Currency Concerns

Currency concerns always exist, but when you buy in a crisis, the local currency will have already suffered substantial losses, depressed by fleeing locals and international investors. Currency markets are more efficient and faster in pricing in economic change, so, actually, you would get another currency discount on top of a price discount for your investment. Now there are cases where currencies continue to drop and a currency reform could possibly occur.

Always remember that you want to hold the ownership rights to any asset. It doesn't matter whether they are traded in local currencies or reformed currencies. A more dramatic scenario would unfold if a new totalitarian government were to annex and confiscate strategic private assets. These cases are extremely rare and haven't occurred within OECD countries.

All currency crises and country crises end eventually, and currency values rise again with economic improvement. Remember to buy ownership rights regardless of old or new currency.

Figure 11.2

	CATEGORY EXAMPLES FOR THE LAST 20 YEARS	
1	1994–95 – 1994 Economic Crisis in Mexico	
2	1995 The Great Hanshin Earthquake	
3	1997 Asian financial crisis	
4	1998 Russian financial crisis	
	1998 Collapse of Long-Term Capital Management	
5	1999-2001 20 year low for key commodities	
6	2001 Dotcom bubble end	
7	2001 911 Terrorist Attacks	
8	1999–2002 Argentine economic crisis	
9	2002-2003 Japan's Banking crisis	
10	2007-2009 US Subprime mortgage crisis	
11	2010-12 European sovereign debt crisis	
12	2011 Tōhoku earthquake and tsunami	
	NEXT: ??? - TO BE CONTINUED!	
	SUBPRIME AFTERMATH - PICK YOUR COUNTRY	
	2009 United Kingdom bank rescue package	
	2008–2009 Belgian financial crisis	
	2008–2012 Icelandic financial crisis	
	2008–2009 Russian financial crisis	
	2008–2009 Ukrainian financial crisis	
	2008–2012 Spanish financial crisis	
	2008–2011 Irish banking crisis	
	2009-Open - Greek Sovreign Debt crisis	

Category Nr. 4 - Single industry and asset class depression

When the dotcom bubble roared between in 1998 and 1999, and Henry Blodget, then legendary equity analyst at Merril Lynch, put his famous buy recommendation on Amazon.com that moved the stock 128% upwards within three weeks, only a few people noticed certain asset classes trading at historically depressed prices. Among them was Jim Rogers, author of *Investment Biker: Around the World with Jim Rogers*, *Adventure Capitalist: The Ultimate Road Trip*, and *Hot Commodities: How Anyone Can Invest Profitably in the World's Best Market*. He had already loaded up on various commodities as early as 1998, when the majority owned investment names ending with .coms in their portfolios, because he recognized that commodities were not only out of fashion, but were trading at ridiculously low price levels relative to the economic development in some emerging markets, including China.

On his second circumnavigation of the globe between January 1999 and January 2002, Rogers researched many emerging markets from his position on the ground. He saw, and was confirmed, that economic changes were coming to Brazil, Russia, India, China, and South Africa, even before the BRICS acronym was coined in 2001. Travelling in his custom-made yellow Mercedes SLK, he further confirmed that he was on the right path to making long-term investments in all major commodities, including agricultural commodities. This was old-fashioned, on-the-ground research that looked into areas where other people didn't dare or were too complacent to look.

Due to his own research and diligent studies of financial history and commodity cycles, Rogers realized that he was onto something that seemed to be almost too good to be true - a real no-brainer. But there it was, in 1999, you could buy crude oil for less than $20 a barrel. In 2008, oil reached its peak of about $140 per barrel. It's the same story with gold. You could buy gold for under $300 in 1999, and it reached its peak in 2011 at $1,921 an ounce. These opportunities are very rare and actually easy to spot. I remember clearly when I asked veteran brokers in 1999 (I was a young banking apprentice then) whether it would be a good time to buy oil or gold. They scoffed at me, arguing these were dead assets.

So if all the people you interview, especially professionals, dislike an asset class, start looking at and researching this particular asset class to prepare for potential no-brainer investments. One could call this contrarian investing, but it is not and I will explain this later. As of my writing this, crude oil and silver have again reached price levels where the majority of existing investors seem to have given up holding onto it, and bought at much higher prices in the hope that the bull market for these commodities would continue a bit longer. Today, they see their horrendous book losses every single day as a reflection of the speculative failure. Not a nice situation to be in. To make things worse, the same professionals who recommended to buy gold in 2011 at peak prices are now recommending to stay away from gold in 2015 at prices of around $1,100, because they forecast it could go down further. You hear similar comments about oil.

Just not loved anymore

Occasionally, a single industry or single asset class gets depressed. Sometimes due to scandals (e.g., in the food industry), or they simply fall out of favor with institutional and retail investors alike. Then there are cyclical industries. When the weakest companies within the industry start going bankrupt, usually due to over-leverage, mismanagement, and lack of support from banks, it is time for expert 80/20 Investors to do some detailed research and to get their cash ready for investments in the strongest and most profitable companies within the industry in question. In 2015 it would have been mining companies and commodity related companies, even though we haven't seen bottom prices yet. You should start looking at the three-to-four industry leaders, or search for industry index funds, and keep them on your watchlist.

Again I would like to warn you that this requires additional research work, a personal inclination, and a better understanding. Don't buy in a single industry simply because it has fallen in price. You still have to use your brain to create a circle of competence around it.

For example, as of writing this, the mining and oil related companies have gone through some terrible months of operating losses, tough questions from creditors, and share price losses. Where the end is, I don't know, and neither do experts. I am personally not a fan of mining companies, in part because it is outside my circle of competence, so I stay away from them, but that is my preference. I know plenty of people who love mining companies and have studied and followed them for years.

Fund managers as a special asset class

This brings me to an investment class that has some special features. Leading fund managers who have proven to have exceptional investment skills, investment acumen, and a wealth of business and economic experience, occasionally suffer their own performance armageddon. Whether Munger in 1973/1974 with his private partnership, Bill Miller of Legg Mason, Mohnish Pabrai of Pabrai Funds, or Bruce Berkowitz manager of the Fairholme Fund, the list of star managers having their own challenging moments in history is endless. Challenges here means moments with terrible performance that spook even their most loyal investment clients.

Extremely capable investment managers all have their down years and, with clockwork predictability, they have panic sellers even among their most loyal investment clients, which worsens their situation even more due to redemption calls and forced liquidations. Even the juggernauts of professional investing can't escape powerful market gyrations or their own occasional failure. But with the same predictability, they recover with some astounding performance comebacks. They become an investment opportunity as part of a shunned asset class that represents no-brainer ideas.

If you consider the Berkshire Hathaway shares price performance, you could recognize the same pattern. In their 50 year history, there have been countless moments where investors got cold feet or were forced to sell their precious Berkshire shares, causing the price to drop even further. These were the moments for entry points to establish a great position in Berkshire Hathaway. 80/20 Investors with cash reserves loaded up on Berkshire shares, because they knew these have been very rare entry points to build a position in the company at fair or even great prices.

If you have always dreamed of giving your money to a star fund manager, but couldn't, a performance crises is a perfect opportunity to invest. Star fund managers are usually closed to the public due to strong demand from investors, but in a performance crises they usually accept new funds to balance out the money outflow of fleeing clients trying to cut their losses. There will be a very high chance that they repay your trust and confidence with future outstanding performances.

Category Nr. 5 - Single company crises

"The key requirement here is that the enterprising investor concentrate on the larger companies that are going through a period of unpopularity. While small companies may also be undervalued for similar reasons, and in many cases may later increase their earnings and share price, they entail the risk of a definitive loss of probability and also of protracted neglect by the market in spite of better earnings. The large companies thus have double advantage over the others. First, they have the resources in capital and brain power to carry them through adversity and back to a satisfactory earnings base. Second, the market is likely to respond with reasonable speed to any improvement shown."

—BENJAMIN GRAHAM, THE INTELLIGENT INVESTOR

The single company crisis is the most common and frequently recurring category for presenting potential no-brainer opportunities. However, benefiting from it requires much more time, effort, experience, financial knowledge, and appetite for risk.

This category is more for the active, rather than the passive, 80/20 Investor. It will be discussed as one of the main topics of my forthcoming book for more advanced investors. For all passive investors, I recommend staying within category one to four.

How to find promising leads?

If you want to find an opportunity in any of the previously mentioned categories, plus your own circle of competence, don't go further than reading your local and leading national newspapers. Whether you're looking for a global financial crises, local economy of foreign country crises, or even single company crises, you will find it on the front page of the business section. There is absolutely no need to subscribe to any of the expensive newsletters or financial news providers. Just keep on reading what you have been reading for years. Keep your eyes open, and a treasure chest will reveal itself.

Action summary of all idea sources

- First, look for no-brainer ideas within your direct or extended business circle and sphere of interest. Use your own circle of competence or passion as your lead advantage.
- Already know what assets or particular investments you want to buy in advance. Through competence and preparedness, you will have more confidence buying your favorite assets when the time comes.
- The best and easiest source of no-brainers is to let the market come to you, rather than forcing something upon the market. In all categories mentioned above, you know that opportunities occur like clockwork.
- In a larger and prolonged economic crises, you can buy anything. The default positions are cheap, broadly diversified, index funds. Alternatively, choose the asset class that you personally prefer and have the strongest circle of competence in. If your personal preference is real estate, research the valuation levels and commit your cash.
- If you prefer to let your money be managed by excellent professionals, such as Mohnish Pabrai, Tweedy Brown or Longleaf Partners, now is the chance to invest. Hell, you could even buy Berkshire shares. Remember that in a real crisis, all assets are equally affected by panic selling, and that includes listed securities, investment funds of excellent investment managers.

- The more specific the crisis is, the more foodwork it requires from 80/20 Investors to drill down on the numbers, to do a thorough analysis, and complete the background checks necessary to gain more confidence.
- Usually, a crisis takes place over an extended period of time, sometimes even years. There is no need to worry about missing the perfect entry point. (More on this in the portfolio management chapter.)
- You don't have to take part in any crisis if you don't feel comfortable, or if it is outside your circle of competence. These are only starting points to search for no-brainer ideas and get your cash ready.
- If a crisis affects a country you know nothing about, and you don't want to do some research on it, stay away! If it is your own country and you are a passive, conservative investor, buy a broad diversified index fund at the best average price you can get.

Nowadays, you can buy index funds for all countries, industries and commodities, and precious metals. You can also buy listed real estate trusts which pay out dividends from rental income with some tax benefits attached (REITs). And, of course, you can invest in your favorite fund managers if they are open for new investors.

However, you should only buy if you feel comfortable holding your positions for the long term, and intend to add to positions in case prices drop further. Naturally, this can only work if you are familiar with the country, industry, or did some intensive study.

Don't commit your money if you don't know anything about real estate as an asset class, even if everybody is telling you to do so. You can become the classic patsy at the poker table. Study it rigorously, do on the ground research, and read about the history of real estate in the area you are intending to do your investing. If you don't feel comfortable making a commitment, take a pass, stay away from this type of investment, and wait for another opportunity to come that is within your personal circle of competence.

The last two categories mentioned here certainly require additional work effort, and more technical skills from a passive 80/20 Investor, but common sense rules hold, and the profit potential more than compensates for the additional work.

CHAPTER 12:
Practice Focus Portfolio Management

Portfolio management is a central part of your investment management system, that gives you a centralized overview of all the separate asset portfolios or special purpose portfolios you might have. From here you can plan, organize, and execute investment decisions as well as maintain existing investments. Like everything else in 80/20 investing, loss protection is the highest priority. For 80/20 Investors, portfolio management is just another tool to reduce and manage risk.

Portfolio management should provide a framework for avoiding, controlling, diversifying, and of course, accepting investment risk. It gives us a structure that, even with an occasional loss, market crash, or financial crises, keeps you steady on your 80/20 investment path. After this chapter, you will be familiar with the concept of base portfolios, how to coordinate and manage them, how you can achieve efficient diversification, and how to buy and build a position. Finally, I will discuss possible reasons for selling. As usual, you'll want to make use of the 80/20 principle to guide you by following the motto "less is more."

Cash portfolio

You need a rock solid framework for portfolio management, and it starts with your cash portfolio, which is considered a base portfolio. This is the key portfolio for attaining financial freedom, which underlies the 80/20 principle. Cash management, as you have seen in Chapter 8, and handling investment holdings are both part of portfolio management and cannot be separated. Everything starts with a money-making engine that generates the cash that feeds your future investments.

The initial cash savings will be held in your cash portfolio. From this portfolio, you can start building up a secondary portfolio -- the investment portfolio.

This portfolio holds your various investments, ranging from listed securities, such as stocks and bonds, to real estate or other ownership rights. For the sake of simplicity, we will focus on a portfolio of listed securities. Listed securities purchased through reputable brokers are deposited at a leading custodian bank in your name for safekeeping.

The cash portfolio will continuously grow with each passing month and with each additional cash contribution. This continues until a no-brainer situation occurs, and your cash is being used to fund a purchase decision. However, and this is important to note, it will replenish itself from fresh cash contributions, which will be generated from your cash engine in the months that follow, as discussed in Chapter 9.

Figure 12.1: Replenishing Cash Portfolio

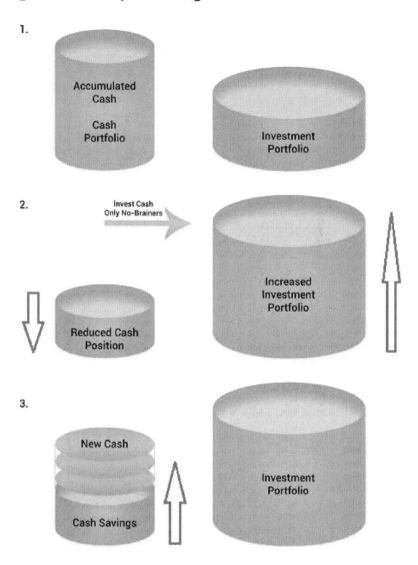

From an administrative point of view, you can deposit your cash with any reputable bank that doesn't charge you too much and that gives you easy access to your cash in case you need to act. Most banks in Western countries offer deposit protection to a certain limit, so consult with your local bank on this matter. In case you go over these pre-set limits, spread your cash over several banks.

Use an Excel spreadsheet, your favorite app, or a notepad to keep track of your cash positions. For this process, there is no need for complicated or expensive software. Refrain from depositing too much cash with brokers, as they usually don't offer the same protection as banks do. Usually, interests earned on cash would also make a difference, but both leading banks and brokers currently don't pay meaningful interests in most G7 countries.

Those who do offer better rates should be treated with caution. They most likely borrow short-term and lend long-term, the worst and most amateurish mistake any financial institution could make. Worse, they speculate with your money in financial markets to attain the yields necessary to attract funds from naive savers.

Portfolio management work effort

Your investment portfolio should follow the 80/20 principle -- "Less is more!" There is no need to mirror professional portfolio managers' work habits. This applies both to the tools you will be using, and most important, the number of different investments you will make.

As an entrepreneur, you might be able to comprehend how extremely difficult it is to create a profitable and growing business. In a competitive world, it requires dedication, commitment to excellence and willingness to constantly adapt to market changes and technological innovation.

You would understand that truly outstanding investment opportunities are extremely rare, so your own portfolio should reflect that fact with only a few truly outstanding investment. Therefore, practice "Focus Portfolio management" focusing only on the so-called no-brainers.

The investment industry is touting hundreds of ideas every single day, but with each buying decision, you not only decrease the quality of each investment, but you also add risk, while doing unnecessary work in the form of decision making and maintenance.

The more investments you make, the more research is necessary to maintain your knowledge base and maintain confidence about all your holdings.

From a portfolio management point of view, the ability and willingness to say "no" to any investment idea is a convenient way to save you from unnecessary work. It will also help you reduce mistakes in investment decisions.

The motto is less admin work, but better investment decisions. Therefore the default answer to the vast majority of ideas you have should be "no!"

The Step-In Plan - A few trades for your Portfolio

Once you identify a no-brainer idea, you need to take action. Don't worry if you miss a perfect entry point. Try to spread your purchases over several weeks and if necessary, over several months. This is what I call a "step-in" plan. All the large investors like Buffett or the Chandler brothers do it. They are just too big to execute one position in one trade without upsetting the price or revealing their identity.

When the Chandler brothers built up their position in Japanese banking shares, it took them about five months, from 2002 to 2003, to establish large minority positions in banks such as Mizuho or UFJ Bank. Warren Buffett took several months when he secretly bought Coca Cola in 1988, eventually purchasing up to 7% of the company for $1.02 billion. [61]

They are never worried about ideal bottom prices, or ideal top prices for that matter. They understand a decent average price is key to future investment success.

Use a step-in buying plan, i.e., buy in several steps. When you buy a no-brainer for your portfolio, decide how much of your cash you want to invest. Commit a sizeable amount of your cash, especially when you buy index funds of your own country. You may not be able to buy a minority stakeholder position in a national Asian bank, or international beloved beverage company, with your first few investment decisions, but that's ok. Everyone has to start somewhere! Let your confidence in the no-brainer guide you.

Divide your allocated cash into tranches, or what I like to simply call "steps", which will give you several bullets for your magazine. I would suggest you split up your allocated cash into, let's say 10 tranches (steps) that you could ideally use for buying over ten weeks.

The smallest purchase amount is usually your first purchase step. From personal experience, and from other 80/20 Investors, we know that we usually buy too early and sell too early. With your first purchase, you aim to test the waters. You can then decide whether to buy again when the price has fallen by, let's say, more than 3%, or wait for a couple of days between your next purchase.

This intermission can function as a cool down period that gives you time to read up on your investment and collect more data. You repeat that process until you have used up the cash dedicated to your new investment position.

Keep in mind that a real, prolonged crises can take years to fully develop, as the Great Depression or the oil crisis in the 70s did. During those periods, financial asset prices fell to such low prices levels that investors today chuckle just imagining such a scenario. I have seen such circumstances with my own eyes in 1997 during the Asian crises and between 2008 and 2009 for several months. I couldn't believe it, and I hesitated to buy in full with each passing month with plenty of my own cash in place -- a big mistake in retrospect.

In case it takes years instead of months, keep on buying with your own monthly cash flow from your cash engine. This is the one rare opportunity (or season, according to Mr. Womack) to plant the seeds for future wealth in years ahead. Don't stop!

In the past, I have been way too early with my purchases due to overexcitement. I learned the hard way that markets exaggerate not only to the upside, but also to the downside. Since then, I learned to invest with smaller amounts at the beginning of establishing a position. If the prices recovered quickly, I made a small profit, but I was not crying after a lost opportunity. If it continued to drop, all the better for me, because I tend to get very excited when prices continue to fall. That usually gives me the chance to execute more of the 10 buying tranches in quick succession at lower prices and with higher nominal amounts of cash to invest that give me an even lower average purchase prices. I start to slow down my purchases when prices seem to bottom out, or even recover, which leaves my tranches a bit smaller at the end.

You will never be able to execute the perfect step-in purchasing plan - it really doesn't matter. It doesn't matter whether you start buying into falling prices in the beginning of a crisis, or continue buying when there are signs of a turning point and prices start recovering. Transaction costs for simple index funds or stocks are so low nowadays that buying several times over an extended period is a viable strategy for even the smallest investment amounts. It doesn't damage your long-term performance, as it used to before internet brokers.

The above mentioned percentages and limits are just guidelines. You need to decide for yourself with each investment and each specific situation. There is never a one-size-fits-all solution. Aiming for a reasonable average price for all your purchases is of utmost importance. I never understood why people use all their cash in one trade just to get done with it. Don't do this. Rather, spread your buying in several steps instead as described above.

Aim for efficient diversification

Diversification is another layer of risk protection. In case your circle of competence fails you (it happens to the best of us), your no-brainer turns out to be less obvious than you had anticipated, or the margin of safety reveals itself to be hot air, you still have another layer of protection within your risk management arsenal: efficient diversification.

Diversification comes back to the original definition of risk: the chance of loss. The main purpose of diversification is to protect us from an absolute catastrophic fallout that will wipe out one of our investments. If you have an efficiently diversified portfolio, such an event would not sink the entire portfolio, because the chances are almost zero that all of our investments will go to zero at the same time. You can ignore all scientific theories on portfolio diversification because their main assumption of risk is market risk, or the volatility of price movement. As we already discussed in Chapter 4 on the principles of risk, price volatility is not the type of risk 80/20 Investors are concerning themselves with.

How diversified you need to be depends on your confidence level in each investment. Your confidence level reflects how securely you are established within your circle of competence. Some diversification is always necessary, but that will never be a problem for 80/20 Investors, because they always have cash as default asset. Besides, over the lifetime of your investment career, you should be able to add all sorts of excellent no-brainer investments to your portfolio, depending on what the markets offer you. These can be stocks, index funds, commodities, private business opportunities, or real estate. It doesn't matter, as long as they are no-brainers. This natural process alone will give you all the diversification you need.

Passive investors usually buy leading index funds, which, by themselves, are well diversified, have very low transaction costs, and are transparent. A traditional index fund usually contains at least 30 of the leading companies in a country, and usually, much more. Examples would be S&P 500 or Nikkei 225 that contain hundreds of leading companies. One index fund in the portfolio is more than enough diversification for a conservative investor. Maintaining this investment portfolio is extremely cheap and simple!

On hedging - avoid it

Nowadays, financial service institutions offer all sorts of sophisticated hedging techniques to eliminate and reduce risk, or so they claim. They recommend derivatives structures such as options and futures, so that if your portfolio decreases in value, the purchased derivatives positions will compensate these losses, because they should move in the opposite direction. At least that is what brokers will tell you.

Common hedging techniques aim to reduce market price volatility, but they can't protect you from simple overpayment risk.

I don't recommend hedging techniques. These techniques have little or no value for the passive 80/20 Investor. Besides a substantial cost (hedging is not free), it increases the workload and overcomplicates the entire decision making process and cuts any profit potential as well. In some cases, it even tempts investors to speculate on certain price movements.

On selling vs. holding

Whatever professionals or investment gurus might tell you, for 80/20 Investors, investment success derives from the buying decisions, not selling. The buying is part of the vital 20% of the equation, the selling part is not. If you made a great purchase at a reasonable price, or a mediocre purchase at a fantastic price, selling will take care of itself.

Mr. Womack is an example of this philosophy. He understood that during depressed markets, if you can get a decent average price at a bottom price range, it would make the selling part much easier, even if you misjudged the timing of the sales.

To clarify, as the market rises, he could sell too soon and make a profit, sell close to the top and make a perfect profit, or sell on the way back down and still make an adequate return. With so many selling scenarios in your favor, paying most attention to the buying price and getting the best possible average price should be your priority and one of the most important tasks as an 80/20 Investor. The magic categories previously discussed are the best starting points.

Returning to the matter of selling, ideally, an 80/20 Investor wants to be a long-term holder in any investment, because a no-brainer opportunity is extremely rare and valuable. Also, internal compounding returns at the company level or reinvested dividends only accrue over time.

It's less work to just hold your investments for many years. Let the power of compounding do its work, while you watch it grow. Mr. Standingback referred to this situation as seeing "a wonderful team of artists doing their amazing job over time." Ironically, he continued following Apple's business development, even though he sold his shares a long time ago.

This process is very similar to keeping your most valuable existing clients versus trying to acquire new ones. It is simply more profitable and less work to keep the good ones. Also, you don't want to end up making a "good enough profit" for a short period of three or six months in the hope you will find another one quickly and end up sitting on your cash again, or worse, invest in mediocre ideas while you could be generating outstanding compound returns for much longer periods from your best investment ideas. Mr. Standingback would whole-heartedly agree on this one.

However, it is critical to know and remember why you have made an investment in the first place, and to sell when signs tell you to act. The work involved in selling is very limited and simple. Once you have made a decision, there is not much you can do or should be doing. The easiest way to maintain a good understanding of any of your investments is to check back every quarter or every six months directly at the source, in case of real estate and single company investments, or, for simplicity's sake, check on some related indices that are published in major newspapers.

Don't get overly fixated on newspaper headlines and their doom and gloom. If you remember from the opening story, Mr. Womack used exactly the same technique to avoid panicking. Most of the time he forgot about his investment for years and occasionally read some newspaper headlines to see how it was faring. Three or four years later, when the stock market was roaring again, and experts were talking about new record highs, he would sell his whole package. When in doubt, just keep your holdings.

In reality, there are only a few situations you should consider selling rather than holding.

- You made an obvious mistake
- The stock market is ridiculously high -- overvaluation
- Personal emergencies
- You are forced to sell
- You feel very uneasy and uncomfortable

There could be many more reasons for you to sell, but these are the obvious ones and easy to remember:

Your made a mistake

It's obvious if you made a mistake -- this applies particularly to single stock type investments. For example, say you bought a company that is involved in an accounting fraud and embezzlement scandal or you just saw that the company has a massive debt position you had initially overlooked. In this scenario, an instant realization should urge you to reconsider your buying decision. If you overpaid for an investment, there will be no help, excuses, or fake arguments that support your initial investment decision. It is time to be honest with yourself -- sell. To a lesser degree, this rule also applies to index funds and countries you have no real knowledge of. Nevertheless, it's really difficult to make mistakes with cheap index funds in a country you know and believe in.

Personal Emergencies

If there is a personal emergency in the family, illness and associated medical expenses have absolute priority. What is the use of money when you or your loved ones are seriously ill and need emergency funding? Remember there will always be new funds coming in month after month.

Bubble Territory

I used to sell much too early, but I have gotten better at this one. In buying or selling, you will never be able to attain perfect timing. An excellent indicator of bubble territory is when everybody is talking about easy stock market gains.

Consider the story of Joe Kennedy, father of President John F. Kennedy, who was an extremely successful entrepreneur and investor. He liquidated all his stock positions right before the crash of 1929 after a shoeshine boy gave him some stock tips. He understood that when even the shoeshine boys have tips, "the market is too popular for its own good." [62] This is a theory that Bernard Baruch, economic advisor to U.S. Presidents Woodrow Wilson and Franklin D. Roosevelt, supposedly swore by, too. He described the scene before the big black Tuesday:

"Taxi drivers told you what to buy. The shoeshine boy could give you a summary of the day's financial news as he worked with rag and polish. An old beggar who regularly patrolled the street in front of my office now gave me tips and, I suppose, spent the money I and others gave him in the market. My cook had a brokerage account and followed the ticker closely. Her paper profits were quickly blown away in the gale of 1929." [63]

These are entertaining stories, and they should be taken with a grain of salt, but they do serve the purpose of illustrating an important point.

Forced selling

You should never be forced out of your situation due to poor liquidity management, because your position of strength can easily turn into a position of weakness. Ever taken part in a liquidation? Bargain hunters love situations where banks have foreclosed assets or have sent people into personal bankruptcy.

You should avoid using financial leverage or bank loans to buy financial securities unless it's legally attached to a specific asset such as real estate. Even then, you should be using conservative finance plans. You don't want to cut it close like many did heading towards the subprime crisis between 2008 and 2009. For the 80/20 Investor, there is no need to use excessive leverage. That's why you have a recurring cash portfolio for our monthly savings, interest, and investment return contributions.

However, there might be situations where you are forced out of your investment due to corporate events such as takeovers and mergers, or going private transactions, when a publicly listed company decides to go private again, as Dell Computers did in 2013. Take this setback with decorum, receive your cash, keep it in your cash portfolio, and wait for the next opportunity. A proxy fight or even becoming a private investor in a new entity is not worth your work and time -- especially for individual investors.

Listen to your intuition

The last reason is more complex and challenging. Selling might give you peace of mind and that's what 80/20 Investing is all about -- "to improve our quality of life through smart investing." It is not worth the self-imposed agony if you end up torturing yourself through sleepless nights just to hold on to an investment. Sell it and get back to your normal life.

There are times when one investment dominates your entire portfolio, because it has outgrown all other investments you own. This is very positive and actually not a real issue. However, if you feel uncomfortable with such a large position in your portfolio, you could consider reducing it and keeping the proceeds in cash. It will reduce the reliance on one single investment and will fill your cash position for possible new opportunities down the road.

In a different situation, it is an intuitive understanding that something has fundamentally changed about your investment and investment rationale. It may be a structural change or a management change you don't like. Whatever it is, if you feel uncomfortable -- sell.

Such investments should be in your circle of competence, so you will have a better understanding than anybody else.

For example, people ask me about Eastman Kodak's slow disintegration and financial struggle. Let me tell you that people at Kodak knew where the wind was blowing. The decline in sales of photographic film and its slowness in transitioning to digital photography was no surprise to anybody who studied it intensively or was directly involved. Listen to your intuition and sell, or even better, don't invest in it at all.

Selling in steps - the Step-out Plan

Selling in steps is very similar to your step-in buying plan, and you should have a "step-out" selling plan. Remember, large investors have to use liquidity to sell their large positions without upsetting market prices or revealing their identity. Hence, they always sell too soon and never receive peak prices. The average selling price counts. Large investors need to think several months ahead before they act with their selling program. They need to decide in advance which investment they want to keep through a potential downturn and which ones they are willing to sell and take profits from. Tax considerations are less important than more sentimental attachments.

For the passive 80/20 Investor, I recommend selling in several steps, in the same way you make new investments. This time, fewer steps are necessary, but your first trade should again be your smallest amount. Remember, there is a tendency to buy too early and sell too early.

Action summary

In portfolio management, keep the following key concepts in mind:

- Manage your cash and investment portfolios separately, but have a simple overview on a sheet of paper or spreadsheet.
- Your cash portfolio should replenish with each passing month.
- Simplify your portfolio management process by doing less.
- Your buying is much more important than your selling.
- When you buy, aim to use your available cash regardless of portfolio percentages or diversification concerns.
- Diversify efficiently -- it is a natural process determined by the availability of no-brainers and cash flow additions.
- Rarely should you be selling. Let the compound effect work for you.
- Maintain your positions the easy way. Check back every quarter or biannually.

- If you feel uncomfortable for whatever reason -- sell!
- Buy and sell in several steps over a period of time to achieve satisfactory average prices.

No matter where you choose to get started, your portfolios will evolve over time and it should display a respectable collection of no-brainers.

Please have a look at the case studies in the Appendix and also read through my FAQ section for additional questions left out in this chapter. Visit my website NomadicInvestor.com to see some real, up to date case studies and market comments, and to check out the 80/20 Investor's Model Portfolio for you to study and follow.

CHAPTER 13:
Beware of Investor's Psychology

"We shall say quite a bit about the psychology of investors. For indeed, the investor's chief problem and even his worst enemy is likely to be himself."

—BENJAMIN GRAHAM

A short story of the American Consumer

The typical American is in debt. Based on an analysis of Federal Reserve statistics and other government data, the average household owes $7,529 on their cards; considering only indebted households, the average outstanding balance rises to $16,140 in 2015 according to NerdWallet. [64]

Americans start getting into debt early on, either through credit cards or student loans. A logical consequence of this is to find a job at any price to pay off the debt accumulated in early years. There is no room for asking themselves what they really want to do in life or what they really aspire to be -- they have already become slaves to the debt spiral that will control their future.

Accustomed to debt, the mental barrier to accumulating more debt is lowered even further. Debtors take out more credit card loans to finance all the goods they think they need and deserve: cars, large TVs, and all those luxury consumer goods they feel entitled to. Add a mortgage to this and its original meaning, "death pledge," becomes reality. With all this debt accumulated over the years, consumers will be in a tight corset of debt repayment and debt restructuring plans. They are forced to make payments on their houses, cars, and credit cards, leaving little room for actually enjoying their lives.

The people who have a tendency for more risks start gambling. People in debt usually dream more of the big lottery wins, the casino prize money, or stock market speculation gains than people who don't have debt. They are the typical suckers for scams, risky deals, and foolish gambling. These people are, according to Richard Russell, "the guaranteed losers."

And because indebted people usually feel forced to make money quickly, they ignore the principle of money, investing, and risk that we discussed in Chapter 4, so they constantly overpay and keep on losing money. They have completely lost control and they can't escape the vicious cycle of debt and its psychological consequences. That's the average US consumer.

Understanding yourself

In money management and investing, you need to free yourself from conventional herd thinking. At the same time, you must understand your own nature and how you behave under pressure, in groups or by yourself. What is your personal relationship to money and risk?

The area I am talking about is psychology. Unfortunately, in academia and general finance education, that field is still given less attention than it deserves.

Why you know it, but still ignore it!

On a regular basis, individual investors rob themselves of all the strength and advantages they have over professionals by giving in to their psychological shortcoming. I know from personal experience how this feels and how powerful these shortcomings are in decision making.

At the risk of repeating myself, every investor's goal is to buy an investment at a low price and then sell it at a higher price. Buy low and sell high! The one thing that always keeps you from accomplishing this simple mission is yourself, not because making the purchase or sale is difficult to find out or to accomplish. You are your own worst enemy, as Benjamin Graham masterfully summed it up in the quote above.

Human instincts and emotions regularly override calm and rational decision making. This topic alone could fill libraries. Factors such as greed, impatience, and fear influence our decision making. Add to this peer pressure and the feeling of having to make money quickly due to debt, and you can see that investing can be emotionally demanding.

Most of my readers must have experienced these emotions themselves, either worrying and fearing for their assets, jobs, and wealth in the bust between September 2008 and March 2009, or when they actually participated in the house-flipping contest that took place before Lehman went belly up.

Here is a common list of investor's emotions you should be aware of, and some useful tips and counter-measures to get in control of them, rather than being controlled by them.

Greed is good?

The most common emotion in investing is greed. It makes us succumb to wishful thinking. For example, naïve investors calculate their potential profits in advance, projecting success after success, and supposing themselves rich with imaginary and totally unrealistic assumptions and profit projections. When these imaginary projections seem to align with real outcomes, the naïve investor's confidence is reinforced, but when fantasy no longer matches the reality, and losses are substantial, the investor experiences a rude awakening.

Greed is also part hubris, that outrageous arrogance, which makes us feel invincible. It is the feeling that nothing could harm us and that the current favorable circumstance will continue forever. Investors that succumb to greed also fall victim to excessive risk taking, which equates to gambling. They use options or futures or simple financial leverage (buying on margin) in cases where they shouldn't have -- just in the hope of magnifying potential gains. In the end, only their losses are magnified.

Impatience - nothing is more painful

"You take it on faith, you take it to the heart, / The waiting is the hardest part."

—TOM PETTY & THE HEARTBREAKERS

Connected to greed is the urge to be constantly active, constantly trading and investing in something, even though the majority of us knows that waiting for a no-brainer would be the more prudent way to achieve positive investment performance. If you asked me what the worst emotion would be in investing, it would be impatience, not greed. The nagging feeling of having to wait for the next opportunity can be an irritating distraction, especially if your cash is growing and growing -- it is an agonizing feeling.

The French polymath Blaise Pascal sums it up in his famous quote, "All man's miseries derive from not being able to sit quietly in a room alone." It's a psychological weakness that affects professional and retail investors alike, but for different reasons.

Where professionals are forced by policies and regulations, along with profit pressure and competitive forces, to invest at all times so as to create that aura of activity, retail investors feel urged on by peer pressure or the simple human urge to gamble. Quite frequently, egos play a dominant role, as investors strive to prove themselves to their social circles at work or at home.

Add to this a large group of people with financial worries, as illustrated by people who are in debt. A natural outcome of this mindset is impatience with money, which causes them to take risks, which for any rational thinking person would be simply titled "dumb".

Fear - a creepy feeling

On the other hand, investors regularly panic in the eye of opposite market movement. Mr. Standingback panicked twice in his investment career. There are many reasons for investors to panic, foremost of which is the realization that they have simply speculated on rising markets without any consideration of overpayment risk.

For many retail investors, the fear of their retirement plans being destroyed due to declining markets makes them sell positions they should actually be keeping. Others start selling wonderful positions because experts convince them to.

As J. Paul Getty said: "a valuable investment secret is that the owners of sound securities should never panic and unload their holdings when prices skid. Countless individuals have panicked during slumps, selling out when their stocks fell a few points only to find that before long the prices were once more rising." [65]

Another effect of fear is failing to buy when buying is the right move. Peter Lynch, former manager of the Fidelity Magellan Fund, writes in *One Up On Wall Street* [66] that, in his estimate, two-thirds of the people who invested in Magellan during the time he managed the fund lost money, even though the fund consistently outperformed the Dow Jones Index while Lynch was manager.

Why? Because they waited until they had seen excellent short-term performance, and then they invested just before the fund started to decline. Shortly before the fund bottomed, they would take their money out and wait until the fund went up before buying again. The total opposite from the "buy low and sell high" adage.

In the end, we all have a very strong instinct of herd thinking. We feel confirmed in our choice to buy when everybody is buying and feel very uneasy holding our assets when everybody is selling.

Establish Protective Mechanism

The old Greeks knew that, ultimately, "wisdom comes through suffering." [67] I fear that it applies to investment success as well.

The urge to buy, especially when everybody else seems to be doing it, and worse, seem to be doing it successfully, is enormous. Professional sales people have long recognized our psychological weaknesses and have taken full advantage of them. I recommend reading Robert Cialdini's *Influence: The Psychology of Persuasion* [68]. His book is a real eye-opener for any consumer.

Talented sales and marketing professionals make use of techniques that appeal to all of our emotions relevant to buying or selling. One classic example is the "limited time offer" that you might be familiar with from TV or internet shopping. Nowhere else more than in investing has this trick had a bigger impact on its consumers. The fear of missing out on a great money-making opportunity, mixed with the urge to be active and to prove oneself to peers, is tempting for anybody who doesn't have a protective mechanism in place.

What is needed is a stable decision framework with the discipline to enforce it. Of course there are no clear formulas for how investors, whether professionals or amateurs, can protect themselves from their own undoing. The ideas listed below are only suggestions to gently guide your own instincts and manage psychological shortcomings. It takes some practice, but over time they will grow on you. Here are my counter measures:

Practice the right mindset

Cultivate and practice a mindset of a wealthy, independent person rather than a person deep in debt. This person operates from a position of strength rather than psychological weakness.

This mindset can be trained and is supported by the principles laid down in this book. Always remember, successful 80/20 Investors don't need financial markets, they just make use of them.

Make use of your personalized checklist. Checklists, as seen in Chapter 9, are a great tool to help organize and systemize your thoughts and decision making process. Add and improve your checklist with every new experience, whether positive or negative.

Make use of your most powerful weapon as a private investor: say "no" to any investment decisions when you are unsure or uncomfortable. Remember, nobody has ever lost money by simply saying "no." The same is true in selling. If you feel very comfortable with your position, because you understand the reasons why you bought it, you are confident it has earnings or earnings potential, and you feel you didn't overpay, say "no" to people urging you to sell.

With your whole investment platform through your other investments, cash portfolio, and cash flow streams, there should never be a reason to be forced to sell. Always remember, "Yes, you can say no."

Make use of your network of like-minded, independent 80/20 Investors. Being accountable to a third party will help you formulate your investment decisions more clearly.

Make use of your free time. Focus on your day job, business, or travel. It will keep your mind calm and protect you from thinking about daily price fluctuations, financial news, and the like. I travel the world, exploring new countries and expanding my chosen circle of competence. Whether it is in spending time learning a new language or studying new industries, countries, or companies, I tend to ignore financial media or price quotation for long periods of time. If you haven't followed them in the past, there is no need to start now -- it won't make you a better investor.

Make use of your past success stories or the success stories of other 80/20 Investors. Use them as success templates and case studies to replicate your investment success for future investments, especially when you had to overcome powerful emotions before. For example, remember the successful situations where you alone were able to take advantage of a great opportunity, ignoring the crowd and conventional thinking, where you were able to see both the forest and the trees, which allowed you to make the right decision. Remember when you were able to raise your fist and point a certain finger gloriously towards Wall Street -- saying: "well, I told you so." These are the moments and case studies that are most likely to protect you from doing something foolish in the future.

CHAPTER 14:
Why it works

"The first principle is that you must not fool yourself — and you are the easiest person to fool."

—RICHARD FEYNMAN

You might ask yourself why this simple investment approach works. Why, with so little effort, was every 80/20 Investor in this book capable of blowing away any professional money manager?

There are three simple reasons:
1. A clear knowledge advantage
2. A self sustaining financial base
3. A structural advantage

Leaving obvious and no-brainer ideas within your own circle of competence aside, you have seen that all 80/20 Investors made active use of the four additional categories -- global market crises, single country crises, individual industry crises or single asset class depression, and single business/company crises. Mr. Womack called this "observing the seasons."

Let me start with a fundamental question: how is it possible that 80/20 Investors can purchase "no-brainer" opportunities at bargain prices, when someone else is forced to sell them? How is this type of outperformance so easy with just a few decisions? Why does the 80/20 way to investing really work? Isn't the market supposed to be efficient according to a key theory of financial academia. [69]

Markets are indeed efficient -- most of the time. But they also behave very irrationally. Market participants make mistakes, big mistakes, and they will continue to do so.

The reasons for this are manifold, but I believe that you have to focus on the area of group psychology, flawed cash management, as well as structural disadvantages hampering large institutional investors that have direct impact on market price developments

Markets are not an intellectual concept that is omnipresent, all knowing, and perfect. The market is made up of real humans, with all their strengths and all their weaknesses. It is the collective psychology of all participants involved, the different investment strategies they follow, as well as their legal and operational structures, which influence the direction of financial markets. This all determines the immediate supply and demand balance that influences market prices in the short-term.

In principle, there are always fundamental and rational reasons for recessions, depressions, profit warnings, or the need for liquidity. But what starts as a result of rational and logical thinking, usually ends up in a frenzy of panic selling that loses all touch with reality and true economic facts. The simple reason for this is that the masses that have long followed the lead of clever investors and market participants, feel forced into ad hoc decisions they weren't prepared for. Too many sellers want out at the same time, and that usually induces more panic selling. The group of sellers are composed of motivated sellers, forced sellers, and of course, short sellers and all the rest who don't understand what's going on.

Here is a list of different types of sellers in a typical panic or stock market decline.

Motivated sellers

Motivated sellers are investors who sell their holdings for mainly non-economic reasons. When indices change their compositions, index funds have to make adjustments in order to remain in sync. They end up selling holdings on a large scale for the simple reason that they need to adhere to their own policies. There were no fundamental or economic reasons to sell.

The largest group of motivated sellers though, is made up of investors who sell for emotional reasons.

The next group of investors only want immediate winners in their portfolios. There are even investment strategies that emphasize this specific point. Feeling uncomfortable due to impatience and increased frustration for being kept waiting (sometime for years), investors start selling, causing increased momentum downward.

Finally, there is the group of market participants that Mr. Standingback always belonged to. They sell out of fear, the fear of uncertainty, the fear that things could get worse, the fear that all their perfect plans will be in shambles. In an unexpected twist of fate, cash suddenly becomes the most attractive asset.

Forced Sellers

Panic selling is the mother of all forced sellers. Someone short on cash, or being forced to liquidate assets in a hurry, has no time to wait for fair pricing. Forced sellers occur in all seasons, but the numbers explode when a panic selling takes place and a real prolonged decline sets in.

The two main reasons for the existence of forced sellers are over-leverage and fund liquidations (Investment funds need to sell their holdings in order to provide liquidity for client's redemption requests).

Even if the owner of the asset knew its real economic value, in these situations there is no choice other than to sell it back to the market in order to get the liquidity he is forced to generate. Waiting for better prices is impossible. This force concerns professional investment managers including hedge funds and all social classes, from the average consumer constantly in debt, to the billionaire who has over-leveraged himself and will go bankrupt in a matter of months.

These situations offer outstanding no-brainer opportunities, especially for 80/20 Investors with heaps of cash accumulated over years. They are usually on the other side of the trades.

Short sellers

Short sellers are a special breed of investors and speculators. With any market weakness or decline, they will be on the frontlines pushing the party forward. They try to profit from market and single stock declines by selling short of their targets, and then trying to purchase them back at much lower prices. They could be short specialists just focusing on this type of trade, or large institutional investors trying to hedge their large portfolios from market declines. Whoever they are, they add momentum to any selling frenzy, making sure that prices overshoot to the downside.

The Reverse Case

We have seen that, thanks to occasional extreme pricing and mistakes committed by market participants, the 80/20 Investor has no shortage of no-brainer ideas, and the liquidity necessary to build even very large positions. But the reverse is true as well.

Eventually, the majority of 80/20 Investors are interested in selling all or part of their assets at much higher prices to return the assets they once bought for bargain prices. Prices might be determined by supply and demand in the short-term, but prices ultimately have to obey the laws of money compounding.

Compounding is the fuel for moving market prices up and, like an oil tanker floating on the ocean, it moves slowly at the beginning but once it has gained momentum it can't be stopped easily. Unlike oil tankers, market prices for all asset classes overshoot regularly -- you know them as asset bubbles. Like the well-known social media effect of "going viral," the momentum attracts more buyers (speculators) in search of easy and quick profits. This brings prices to fair valuation and, most of the time, to extremely high prices. This process can take years, but you know 80/20 Investors are never in a hurry.

Taking Advantage of No-Brainers

The existence and regular appearance of no-brainers is obvious, but this is only one side of the coin. An equally important question is:

why do only a few investors take advantage of them? Why is a person, who bought Apple shares for $9 a share with good reasons and diligent research work, not able to buy the same company at 90 cents a share just a few months later? Imagine what Mr. Standingback's net wealth would look like today if he had kept buying those Apple shares as prices fell and stayed with it, instead of standing-back from the action.

Let me explain in more detail: the secret of 80/20 Investors is that they do things differently than the majority of market participants, especially large institutional investors such as pension funds, mutual funds, or insurance funds, because they can.

Professional management not without side effects

Professional fund managers cannot afford to deviate too much from their respective benchmarks; if they do, they risk extreme underperformance that could be bad for fund sales and hence their personal bonus. The larger the fund in question, the more it resembles the benchmark it is trying to beat, but charging much higher fees.

A side effect of this policy is that fund managers feel forced to buy and sell at any price, just to avoid deviation from their benchmarks. Their individual holdings sizes, as measured by the percentage invested in one single investment, reflect the weightings in their respective benchmarks. That means that one single holding will never have a dominant position over all other investment holdings in a fund. The argument is that the entire fund could be unstable and it doesn't reflect the risk parameters that led customers to choose this particular fund in the first place.

That also means that even if they could identify the next Facebook or Google, they could never invest more than a small percentage of total assets in this particular promising company. It would be against self-imposed compliance and risk rules, and sometimes against regulations.

Another dilemma professionals often face is the justification of paying high prices, even though they know these prices don't make economic sense from a valuation point of view. However, they can't stop their business entirely, go home, and wait for better prices. This dilemma applies to all institutional investment vehicles such as venture capital, private equity or real estate companies. Salaries need to be paid, deals need to continue flowing - normal business life has to go on regardless of high or even outrageous prices. If necessary, an analyst will come up with some self-fabricated statistics to justify investment decisions by managers.

Yes, we can

The 80/20 Investors make full use of their structural advantages and take action. What are their advantages?

The biggest advantage by far is their own sources of funding. They never fear redemptions or forced liquidations -- they always have cash inflows through their own money engine. This gives them the freedom to only focus on the most important tasks that give the biggest bang for the buck. They can afford to wait for their preferred opportunities, even if it takes years.

Figure 14.1: Stay within your own circles

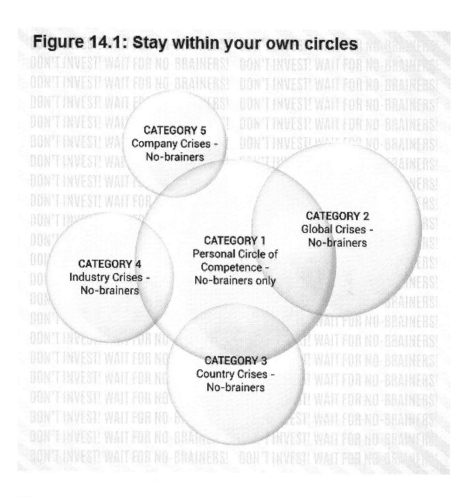

Who cares about stable returns?

Conventional investors dream of stable, near fixed annualized investment returns to match savings rate returns, even though they know that the large majority of the underlying businesses, or asset classes, will never generate predictable and complete stable returns. It is just unrealistic - every business owner understands this. Monthly sales and earnings vary and sometimes widely fluctuate for reasons they are not in control of. Ironically, all professionals money managers are measured against stable recurring monthly and annual investment returns, with the lowest possible volatility in between. This is how major hedge funds market themselves to institutional investors. They do everything, and I mean everything, to achieve stable as possible investment returns, even giving up clear investment opportunities. All institutional investors hate volatility. Tough luck -- volatility is your partner in investing and business, like Laurel was to Hardy or Walter Matthau was to Jack Lemmon. They are inseparable.

80/20 Investors don't mind the volatility in returns. What counts is the final return when they consider selling when they get offered great prices. I know a couple of, what I term "Apple Geeks," who bought Apple shares like Mr. Standingback at similar prices or even better. But instead of selling after 100%, they decided to hold them to this day. You can imagine, these investors don't care much today how Apple share prices traded in 2001, 2009, or even 2012. They know their initial purchase prices and how much value they got for their purchases. That makes them easily forget how Apple trades on any single day today or in the future.

Just look at the Apple stock price chart since 1998. There is huge volatility in performance between each year, but nobody could argue that the annualized compound rate of return is phenomenal, even though Apple suffered like any other stock in 2001 and 2008.

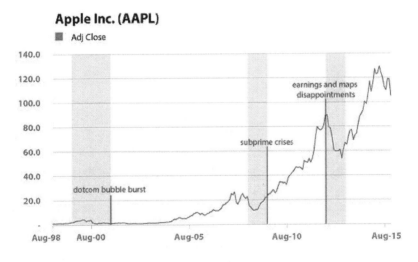

Apple Inc. (AAPL)

■ Adj Close

Close price adjusted for dividends and splits.   Source: Yahoo Finance

Look at Berkshire Hathaway, which suffered so many financial crises and stock market declines in its 50-year history since Buffett took over. None of the first-time shareholders even blinked an eye when they suffered one of several major crises that affected Berkshire's price quotation.

The 80/20 Investors don't compete for returns. They don't have to. They don't feel the pressure to beat neighbors, peers, or benchmarks each week or month of the year, and they don't fight redemptions or cash flow problems. They just have an enormous structural advantage, and they make use of it.

Make use of concentration

Due to the fact that 80/20 Investors make fewer decisions, these decisions are much better in quality and have a bigger impact on performance. Thus, they have the confidence to commit larger amounts of cash. If you consider your strict buying criteria and combine this with higher concentration in the form of capital commitment, you can see that the performance impact on your investment portfolio is phenomenal. If you then add more no-brainer investments over time, funded by additional cash flows, you can see that 7% annualized returns on your invested capital is a very realistic expectation and, as a matter of fact, at the heart of 80/20 Investors expectations.

When Buffett restarted his buying in late 1974, he started with investments he already owned. And why not? Why should you buy something new when you already have great ideas right in front of you that you know inside and out. The result was that a natural concentration took place, assuring the quality of his portfolio composition and very impressive performance results.

Certainly the opposite is true as well, as Munger painfully experienced himself between 1973 and 1974. But compared to many other market participants, he knew exactly what was in his portfolio, and he was very confident that the low prices were due to market forces (panic sellers) and not due to mistakes he made with his investments. Remember, your portfolio is made up of the collection of no-brainers you have identified and that you have the highest confidence in.

In Mr. Standingback's case, the ideal outcome would have been to keep his Apple shares and to add to the same position persistently with each market shock and subsequent price decline. In 2001, Apple declined by almost 90%. Had he added another $10,000, he would have doubled his position at almost the same purchase price. Similar to Mr. Womack who added to his portfolio when prices continued falling in the 1970s. He simply added another $25,000 package, and made a fortune on his whole stock portfolio when the market recovered and set trajectory on a long-lasting bull market.

Mr. Standingback could have done it again during the subprime crises. He could have added to his position between 2008 and 2009. Though at a higher average price, but with even more performance potential. Afterall, the iPhone was just rocking the tech and communications world since June 2007. A natural concentration would have taken place with the full confidence and experience of a person who had watched and studied Apple for more than 10 years.

Are you a contrarian?

People might describe 80/20 investing as a form of contrarian investing.

I disagree.

When J. Paul Getty bought his oil stocks during the biggest stock crises in his decade, he looked like a contrarian investor. He wasn't! The investment rationale behind his purchases of oil stocks was fundamentally different to simple contrarian thinking.

80/20 Investors are not interested in making a point of acting differently than anybody else, like a little boy disobeying his parents. They are buying because all categories offer profitable searching grounds, and because they offer no-brainers.

Everybody would agree that "buy low and sell high" is the essential formula to follow, only 80/20 Investors seem to be able to take full advantage of these rare no-brainer events. The majority of investors follow the mantra to be fully invested at all times, to have minimum or better no cash reserves. Naturally, that leads them to commit money in mediocre investments which they themselves intuitively know are mediocre at best.

80/20 Investors, on the other hand, understand the value of cash reserves and the virtue of patience. They understand this as the "optionality of cash" - a huge structural advantage over all conventional investors. They can hold large amounts of cash, and change from asset class to asset class. If real estate is cheap and offers great rental yields, they buy real estate. If the stock market offers them no-brainer opportunities, they take it with gusto. If gold or silver is unpopular again, they buy at great prices. If everything is ridiculously cheap, they just buy the assets they feel most comfortable with. The Rothschilds laid the early foundation, Hetty Green understood the same principle very early on, so did Carlos Slim and the Chandler Brother, and all the other investors that made use of the 80/20 principle to investing. They took 100% advantage of their freedom, their knowledge advantage, and most important, the availability of cash reserves.

Final thoughts

Some might still disbelieve the radical effectiveness of the 80/20 approach to investing. They think these investors are the beneficiaries of chance and simply overestimate causality.

Unfortunately, these people ignore that 80/20 Investors don't attempt to anticipate the future by trying to impose causalities where none exist (80/20 Investors call this speculating). Rather, 80/20 Investors take advantage of the errors of those who unsuccessfully attempted to anticipate the future based on wrong assumptions and indicators. These market participants usually overpay. In my career, I have heard and read the wildest forecasts, warnings, and market price predictions, that ranged from bizarre to just plain stupid. Astoundingly, a lot of investors bet money on many of these forecasts, with predictably disappointing results. 80/20 Investors wait and pick up the pieces where these punters have failed, and most likely have been fooled by randomness and wrong causalities.

Follow the motto 80/20 Investors swear by: "Don't lose your money! Let the other poor bastard lose his!"

CHAPTER 15:
Are you an 80/20 investor yet?

You are nearing the end of this journey. If you recall the story about Mr. Womack, you will now realize that he, though unaware of it, deployed the 80/20 principle to his full advantage. His investment approach contained all the important elements described in this book as part of the 80/20 Investing approach. It was a simple approach with maximum impact.

All the 80/20 Investors you have met in this book did not worry about market fluctuations, stable returns, or what other experts told them to do. They never wasted their energy on hyperactive trading or unnecessary activities in their investment operations. They just did what appeared natural to them to achieve outstanding returns and with minimum effort.

Consider also that starting with the Rothschilds in the 1800s, all the historic and living 80/20 Investors had to deal with enormous political or economic uncertainties in their investment lives. They were confronted with natural disasters, industrial revolutions, two World Wars, extreme depressions, deflation, stagflation, and hyperinflation. The world was on the brink of a third world war, we have seen interest rates (FED funds) reaching almost 20%, and finally, a global financial system at near total standstill. Investors had to live through all of them, and it wasn't any less complex to assess the uncertainties as it is today.

Yes, we live in an uncertain and volatile world -- we always have and we always will -- but thanks to their unique approach and mindset, all 80/20 Investors have successfully managed to thrive despite uncertainties of their times. They will continue to do so in the future -- and so can you.

Help Mr. Standingback

If you recall the story of Mr. Standingback one last time, who so diligently worked and saved all his life, but somehow always got his timing wrong, you could now offer him a simple and convincing solution to his dilemma.

Imagine if he had just saved, held his stocks, and continued to buy through only two great financial crises he must have experienced in the last 20 years. After stocks corrected sharply, he would have easily achieved financial freedom by now.

He was an excellent worker, capable of saving money to consistently replenish his cash portfolio. He was following one of the 80/20 cornerstones to perfection. However, his ultimate failure was not having a mindset and accompanying investment approach that appropriately reflected his lifestyle and circumstances.

He bought the wrong investments, and he bought at the wrong prices. His fixation on the specific retirement numbers he calculated for himself made him a victim to fear, greed, and impatience. Most importantly, this fixation engendered a sense of urgency where none was needed.

Instead of sticking to an area he understood and felt comfortable with, Mr. Standingback swapped and jumped around without any confidence, just because some so-called experts told him to. In the end, he always panicked when prices moved against him.

What you could offer him as a solution is pure simplicity and common sense -- the essence of the 80/20 way to investing :

- Keep accumulating cash
- Invest big in no-brainers only

ADDING THE CORE 80/20 TASKS

Figure 15-1: Adding the missing Core 80/20 Tasks

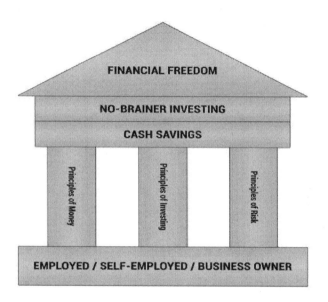

At the beginning of this book I made two assumptions 1) that the best and easiest way to attain financial freedom is through saving and investing, and 2) that saving and investing is simple if you make use of the 80/20 principle.

In a simple three-step process, I have laid out a destination, the tasks necessary, and the action points to be taken by individual investors who want to follow the 80/20 approach.

I have demonstrated that, thanks to the 80/20 principle, saving and investing can be simple, while still using your brain rather than switching off to autopilot completely. You have seen that you can achieve competitive returns with minimum effort while still maintaining your day job, other business endeavors, or hobbies and personal interests.

In this book, you have seen that, without complicated formulas, advanced accounting knowledge, or financial jargon, you can become an independent investor. With the help of what I have set down for you to contemplate, the ongoing research I will publish, you will go on to make better and more confident decisions achieving adequate returns that will help you on your quest to financial freedom. If there is one last thing I want you to remember, the core take away of this book is to always recall Womack's farming advice: obey the seasons, for winter is coming!

AFTERWORD

A lot of people search for specific formulas and detailed instructions to determine their next steps for them instead of determining their own strategy. This book isn't for them. Investing is an individual activity based on individual circumstances and experiences, hence the process of assessing no-brainer opportunities seems subjective and intangible. No formulas, checklists, or principles will ever replace individual, independent thinking.

Investing the 80/20 way is not a magical shortcut to overnight riches. It is a way to reach your investment goals in the most efficient way. The method doesn't guarantee investment success or easy investment returns. You still have to think and make decisions for yourself. This requires effort and discipline.

Having said this, just reading, understanding, and having good intentions to adapt all, or certain parts of this book, will not initiate change in your investing habits. Good intentions are no substitute for positive action.

I can almost hear the many voices of disgruntled individual investors saying, "Why did I have to put my retirement funds in poor performing investment funds with high fees?" or "Why didn't I just wait for a better and more obvious idea"? or, "Why didn't I buy this no-brainer when it was cheap?"

I have also blatantly ignored simple advice from great investors and mentors for most of my investment career, with the misguided idea that I would be able to handle challenging circumstances as they came, that I was different. In retrospect, this was plain hubris. I was dead wrong.

Since then, I've realized that I needed to change my approach and develop a strong desire to listen and to take positive action. That desire came from within, and not from my mentors. Ultimately, I adopted the principles described in this book on my own.

GET YOUR FREE SUPPORT PACKAGE

I am aware, therefore, that I can't change a person's habits overnight with a single book, especially if that person is encumbered with fear or impatience, and is constantly bombarded by contradictory advice, predictions and warnings. Hence, to encourage positive action and to help connect more of the dots, I will publish a series of blog posts, research, books, and maintain a model portfolio at NomadicInvestor.com to showcase and demonstrate the 80/20 investment approach in a real environment and in real time, for you to better understand and to adapt its principles.

In addition to that, all readers have access to the free support package, which includes an action list summary, a sample checklist and some valuable case studies (e.g. The Nikkei 225 challenge).

Enjoy the path to financial freedom

As I write this, I am preparing to visit Greece for a month to study the investment behaviors of Greek entrepreneurs, as well as the Greek real estate and the financial markets, which will be material for my next book project.

I will take this opportunity to fulfill my curiosity about the current state of Greece's economy, the people and country, and its future development. I want to see with my own eyes how this country is adjusting to its challenging circumstances. I plan to meet friends, acquaintances, and hope to make new personal and business contacts and start new conversations, which could lead somewhere. As Steve Jobs said in his famous commencement speech at Stanford University, "Stay hungry, stay foolish." I don't know whether I will ever be able to make use of this experience, but it might come in handy one day -- life is full of surprises.

My way of life wouldn't have been possible if I hadn't come upon the 80/20 way to investing, inspired by Richard Koch, described by Richard Russell, and demonstrated so vividly by Warren Buffett through his own life.

They all inspired me to choose the right path, to choose the work I love doing, to save and to invest the 80/20 way; to become an 80/20 Investor, and I hope you will do the same.

APPENDIX

FREQUENTLY ASKED QUESTIONS (FAQ)

This is an overview of frequently asked questions from individual investors who are just starting out. I would like to address the most common questions and concerns.

Caveat

Investing is not for everyone. As with everything in life, when taking financial action unilaterally, there is risk involved. Foremost is the risk that you will undermine your own effort to attain investment success by mindlessly gambling or not getting your emotions under control.

For people who cannot and do not want to deal with price fluctuations or investment decision making in general, I can only recommend that they adjust their financial affairs accordingly. These individuals should not get involved in any kind of investment operation recommended by their bankers or media.

If you decide against investing in financial assets, keep investing in yourself and your family which would be part of one of the Magic Categories to search for the best ideas.

Here are the most commonly asked questions from my readers:

Do I need a lot of time for my investment portfolio?

Many individual investors have a preconceived notion that investing is enormously complex and requires enormous amounts of time. This doesn't have to be the case . The brokerage firms and mutual funds that dominate the financial industry have nurtured this view. It is in their best interest to make you believe that investing is too hard, takes too much time, and is too risky to do on your own. By applying Pareto's Principle and by mirroring the activities of 80/20 Investors, less than an hour spent per week on average is sufficient to maintain your investment portfolio. You commit capital, in order to let capable people and their business models work for you. I personally have plenty of time to travel the world, collect research for my books and enjoy life. I sometimes don't read news or watch stock tickers for days and even weeks, and neither should you.

Do I need large amounts of capital to invest?

The objective of this book is to grow and solidify your asset base in order to attain financial freedom. Nowadays, you can open a simple stock or dedicated securities portfolio with an online broker with less than $1,000 and add to it on a monthly basis. Over time, while monthly savings and investment returns accumulate, your cash portfolio will grow. Trust me, it will!

Do I need a finance education? Do I have to go to university?

As long as you don't work on Wall Street or manage money for other people, you don't need financial training or a university degree. All you need is common sense, some business sense, and an understanding of your own psychological limitations. If you follow the principles laid down in this book and reread Chapter 13 on psychology several times, you won't need anything else. For more practical and timely examples, encouragement, and inspiration, visit NomadicInvestor.com.

But isn't Investing too risky?

Most people have a wrong sense of risk -- they mix up price volatility with the risk of real loss of capital. Yes, if you invest, you are taking risks, mainly the risk of overpaying for something you don't know anything about. The principles applied in this book are intended to reduce the real risk of capital loss. In the long run, you might even be able to reduce your overall financial risk through smart 80/20 investing. Solely relying on your government and relying on your banker to take care of your retirement is naïve and much riskier. If you can't handle price volatility of financial assets, keep your money in cash and only buy things that represent value to you. First and foremost, invest in yourself, your family, and possibly your own cash flow generating businesses. These are all category I investments.

What type of investments or asset classes should I buy?

When we talk about investments, we talk about anything where you can deploy your cash, protect your capital, and receive an adequate return. Hence, getting more money back than you have initially spent. These investments could be made in yourself, real estate, private businesses, or even art. Besides investing in yourself or your own existing business, I don't know of any other place to find no-brainers on a regular basis, with ease, speed of execution, and with the lowest transaction cost, than publicly regulated exchanges. They offer protection and transparency among buyers and sellers. There is really no need to look anywhere else, unless you are an absolute expert in one specific asset class and have a dominant circle of competence, such as real estate or investing in private businesses.

Remember, if investing in startups, websites, and other private businesses is what works best for you, you have extensive experience in the field, and a competitive edge, by all means, keep doing it until profits run out and you are ready to move on.

For the simplicity of most passive individual investors, I recommend a focus on investments in publicly listed securities (including index funds) as the main source of investment transactions. Our universe is the stocks of individual companies, index funds of whole countries, asset classes, or specific industries (these include real estate or commodities) from reputable index fund companies such as Vanguard or BlackRock.

So I shouldn't use any advisors or pros for help at all?

You still need professionals, and you still need their information and expertise. However, the buying decision is made by you and you alone, based on the investment approach and the categories described in this book.

Professionals will help you go through the tedious paperwork. They can also offer you updates on current market situations and much more, but you decide and you initiate the buying and selling and not the other way around.

For example, say a real estate broker calls you and offers you, according to him, a fantastic property deal. You do some background check and maybe visit the place, and you find out that the plumbing needs a complete overhaul. Obviously not a no-brainer idea -- you simply say no! You should also consider terminating any business contact with this particular broker.

On the other hand, say you've known a property in your neighborhood for a long time, you've just heard that the owner is selling, and the price seems fair. You can use a broker or your agent to do some background checks and research for you, as a means to confirm or critique your initial investment rationale. You let him prepare all the paperwork, and he joins your real estate team as a trusted member. In this case, you are in control of the entire buying or selling procedure, and advisors offer real value to your project team.

Why aren't there more 80/20 Investors -- why isn't this form of investing more mainstream?

The first reason is that the 80/20 principle is counterintuitive among industry professionals and individual investors alike. The majority of investors wrongly believe there is a linear relationship between risk and return, work input and return output. As you have seen from this book, this is just not true.

Another reason is that it doesn't fit into the modern world of finance and fund management, where everything needs to be complex and requires a lot of time so that high fees can be charged.

There are actually quite a few 80/20 Investors and they exist all over the world. But they usually keep a low profile, like the Chandler brothers or even Mr. Womack.

Is the 80/20 way of investing a shortcut?

Some readers might recognize a contradiction, because the 80/20 principle should make our lives much easier. Isn't this the potential shortcut we have been all waiting for? Unfortunately, you won't see magic returns happen just by applying the 80/20 principles. Rather, the principle is a means of reaching your goals in the most efficient way. The process of learning and gaining experience, and, most importantly, the commitment to an 80/20 approach still requires effort from the person who applies it.

This book is about becoming an 80/20 Investor, an approach that promises to focus on only the most effective tasks that bring competitive returns. It doesn't guarantee investment success, nor does it offer an easy and fast shortcut to investment returns. Readers still must commit themselves, and, most importantly, think for themselves. Doing this requires effort and discipline.

Don't I have to do some calculations and valuation sheets?

"People calculate too much and think too little," Charlie Munger once said. As long as you don't buy complex single securities or very complex businesses, you don't need to do any classic valuation works such as discounted cash flow models. The assumptions we usually use to make future predictions in order to value assets are ridiculous and not realistic most of the time.

Even if you bought single securities, by focusing only on "no-brainers," there is no need for extensive valuation work, as the undervaluation or the "cheapness" of an asset should be so obvious that you can do very simple calculations in your head or with a piece of paper and high school math.

I suspect I will be heavily criticized for oversimplifying the process of investing, a subject that is voraciously studied by the most intelligent people in finance and economics. Well, life is simple. As an old Zen proverb says: "Drink your tea, eat your rice, wear your clothes." The whole point of applying the 80/20 principle is to focus on only those tasks that matter the most, and you have seen that there are not many of them. Just because you do very detailed spreadsheet analysis doesn't mean your investment performance will be better.

According to Warren Buffett, "There seems to be some perverse human characteristic that likes to make easy things difficult." [61] Take the complication of the process and you will see the same results, or most likely better results.

What about relative cheapness?

One of the biggest scams to lure investors into investing on Broker's terms is the argumentation of relative cheapness. You might have heard something along the lines that company A is cheap and should be bought relative to company B which is considered expensive within a sector. Popular valuation models used for this argumentations like these are PE or EV/EBITDA ratios I will explain in my book for advanced investors.

Well, in a specific context these valuation tools are valuable and have their place for sophisticated and professional investors. However, these tools are extremely misleading for the laid back investor and most often bluntly abused by vested interest. At any point of time in financial history, something always has been relatively cheap to something else. Despite this, people lost tons of money relying on this argument alone.

During the subprime crises I had readers and friends approached me asking me in confusion and obvious distress, why one particular country or specific stock dropped so much. "David, brokers recommended me this specific stock A, because they swore that this investment is cheap relative to investment B"- I had to buy it" Sadly they lost 40% of their investment and sometimes more. What made it worse is that they actually realized their book losses - only to see them rise again a couple of month later.

Relative cheapness will not protect you from horrendous losses, whether this applies to single companies, industries or entire countries. So, if a broker comes with an investment idea based on relative cheapness - stay away or even better fire him!

Do I have to time the markets?

It's not a question of timing, but pricing. From Chapter 5, you have seen that all successful 80/20 Investors are experts in some fields or another -- they have their own circle of competence and are capable of determining value in their respective fields without much effort. They are capable of distinguishing great investment opportunities, the so-called no-brainers, from a mountain of ideas offered to them on a daily basis. Hence, they know roughly when to buy -- not because they want to time the market searching for bottoms or tops, but rather by the price they pay relative to the value they see they can get. Value here means also the understanding of growth potential, not only pricing tangible assets. All 80/20 Investors know a bargain when they see it -- they don't time bargains.

But I never seem to be able to find bottoms or tops. Is there a convenient way?

Do you remember the story of Mr. Womack and Mr. Hogan? They both came to understand that during a depressed stock market, if you can get a solid average cost price position at the lower price range, it will be sufficient for any future scenario or misjudgments. A good cost price always contains a sufficient margin of safety. If you buy no-brainers at a fantastic price, especially in index funds, then a cheaper price is even better. Keep on buying with your monthly cash flow from your primary cash engine and achieve a good average cost price. Remember, such an instance is one of those rare moments to deploy all your cash and cash revenues. Make maximum use of it and find a new home for your cash.

Thanks to great average cost prices, Mr. Womack and Mr. Hogan knew that during a market rise, they could sell too soon and make a profit, sell at the top and make a very good profit, or sell on the way down and still make a profit. So, with so many profit scenarios in your favor, waiting for the best cost price possible is worth aiming for, and one of the most important cornerstones of 80/20 Investing.

Still not satisfied? For buying, use the simple advice Jim Rogers has been following for years: "You know a market has bottomed out when everybody gives up in despair and does not even want to talk about it." The reverse would also be true, if you recall Kennedy's shoeshine boy story.

But what about asset allocation and portfolio diversification?

Forget about it. If you buy index funds or a basket of industry leaders within an economy or industry (similar to what Carlos Slim did between 1981 and 1982, or what the Chandler brothers did in 2003 with a portfolio of banks) you will get plenty of diversification.

Follow the principle of saying "no." If you don't understand the asset class, you shouldn't be buying it just to have a perfect asset allocation or to look cool to your broker or neighbor. This rule applies to gold and real estate as well. You should not force an artificially designed pie chart on the market, and pay dearly for it.

Remember when everybody was telling you to buy gold at any price in order to have a great asset allocation mix and an inflation hedge? They continued recommending at $1,900 in 2011 and down. Today the same voices recommend selling gold at prices we haven't seen for a long time. After four years, it is trading at about $1,100 in December 2015 -- a minus of 42% (the same counts for silver). It just doesn't pay to follow an asset allocation model that professionals promote so much. I remember when the subprime crisis hit, there was not a single asset allocation model that could have protected you from the malaise. Even money market funds experienced massive losses, which was just bizarre, as money markets should actually be risk free and by definition should be invested in near cash investments.

Your 80/20 asset allocation evolves naturally with the availability of no-brainer investment opportunities and not due to pre-set pie charts based on irrelevant assumptions such as price volatility risk.

Why shouldn't I just buy index funds then?

This route is actually recommended by leading professional investors, who I highly respect, and I do support their views. Passive 80/20 Investors should be buying index funds in the three categories I described in Part III.

However, the fundamental problem with this strategy is the same as for any other strategy: how to determine acceptable buying and selling prices. The industry solution is to establish a monthly savings plan called "dollar cost averaging." The theory behind it is that you don't have to time your buying or selling decisions because your average price and your long-term holding period should reflect the historic performance averages. It doesn't work in a country such as Japan or Greece and, from the looks of it, won't be working very well for many years to come in the US due to interest cycles.

I, personally, am a strong opponent of this naïve, dumbed down strategy. It encourages private individuals to stop thinking entirely and to go on autopilot. Furthermore, it generates unnecessary paperwork and transaction costs, and it robs you of cash resources when you really should be buying when things are cheap to get the best value. Why should you invest a fixed amount of money if you consciously knew that these are obvious bubble prices just to blindly following your own set policy? Why should you buy only a small fixed amount of your index fund, when the market has dropped dramatically? Why would a healthy rational thinking human act against common sense of following a simple rule of buying low and selling high, just because the fund industry promotes it?

Following a dollar cost averaging buying plan, your average returns will most likely be much worse than the index funds themselves. That means, if the index performance is about 7% for the last 10 years, yours will be below it. If you use the 80/20 investment approach, you will do less trading and most likely achieve better annualized returns than the index fund itself.

I have said it before, and I will say it again: investing requires you to think for yourself and to take responsibility -- nobody should do this for you. You can't just transfer thinking completely to someone else or rely completely on someone else's theoretical buying model. Look back at all 80/20 Investors; they would have never thought of doing something as stupid as dollar cost averaging, because they knew how to think independently.

Should I follow a buy and hold strategy?

No, you shouldn't. A simple buy and hold strategy is another form of switching off your brain and foregoing independent thinking. Ideally, you want to keep a great investment that you got a fair price for as long as possible, or, in other words, as long as your investment performs satisfactorily. You want to make use of the compounding effect, which only works over time, and you want to keep your star managers as long as possible or as long as they work for you. But due to the nature of business and its competitive forces, investment valuations are in constant flux. Star managers leave, new managers make terrible mistakes and innovation can destroy even the most established and considered safe industries. Monitor your investment on a quarterly basis or semi-annual basis. Due to your personal expertise, you and only you can tell if there is a fundamental rift happening in your investment. Follow the selling guidelines from Chapter 12.

Should I sell my existing holdings if I find a new no-brainer idea?

Only you, acting within your personal circle of competence, can decide for yourself. The rule of thumb is clarity -- your new opportunity needs to be so obvious that literally a fool couldn't lose on it. From experience, this is extremely rare. Therefore, as a default position, I would recommend you keep your existing investments, especially those that you know in detail, have proven themselves, and you actually like. Use only your newly accumulated cash for a new no-brainer opportunity.

If you have a once-in-a-lifetime opportunity in a private business deal (the next Google or Facebook) -- go for it. Be aware, though, that the next Facebook and Google are extremely rare and the chances of loss of capital are real. In this extreme case, I would suggest you keep at least half of your portfolio in existing investments.

I have moral concerns taking advantage of the suffering of others.

You shouldn't! First, you are not responsible for the economic suffering in the first place. For example, currently I am researching Greek investment opportunities. I am not responsible for the mess the Greek financial elite and the EU themselves have caused for the Greek people. Massive losses in asset prices are a direct result of mismanagement by the assets owners or complete mismanagement by governments and their leading financial institutions. Second, you merely take advantage of other investors who are pressured to make mistakes. Look at it as a transfer from weak hands to strong hands. A cleansing process is necessary for a healthy and strong recovery.

With your capital commitment, you are actually supporting the early sprouts of a recovery. As you commit your saved capital, you are giving back financial resources to be deployed in economic activities of a company or a whole country.

But I want to save on taxes....
I only want to invest in dividend stocks.

This concern is also expressed as: "I want to reduce my taxes so that I can get more money out" or "I only invest for income/dividend purposes, because I want high and stable incomes -- I don't care about the principal invested."

Don't invest exclusively for tax purposes, and don't only invest for dividends purposes. This is, in my view, a foolish mental shortcut. It violates the principles of investing.

Most investors get excited when they hear advisors touting some tax benefits scheme – at least it grabs their attention. Occasionally, they end up investing in some strange countries or investment vehicles, from which their money will never return.

Rather than focusing on optimizing your portfolio for tax benefits, you should always and only invest for investment returns that obey the definition of investing. Protect your capital and require an adequate return. Besides, for most investors, just keeping a great investment for many years has an immense tax benefit without the complications.

It doesn't make economic sense to save 2% from your investment yield if you lose a substantial amount of your invested principal, or worse, all of your capital, which may happen if you get caught in tax saving scams. Occasionally, unproven tax savings schemes will be legally penalized by tax authorities. In such cases,you end up paying more in penalties than you have originally hoped to save in taxes. If you ignore overpayment risk and the risk of scams, no tax saving scheme in the world will be able to make up for the losses. Furthermore, with any complicated tax scheme, you add work and unnecessary advisory fees.

As previously mentioned, if you really want to save some money on reducing your tax payouts -- stop trading around! Keep your investment and reap the benefits of reinvested compound returns. Returns not paid out to you will not be taxed twice, but only at the corporate level, so you reap an additional compound effect by not paying the tax man until the very end of your investment.

For the same reason, a lot of investors are eager to save on taxes, people aim for the perfect dividend-paying portfolio. I understand the benefits and intellectual concept behind it, but the risk of overpaying and the risks of falling prey to fraudulent Ponzi schemes is very high.

Sometimes you read ads that promise payouts of 10% or more on some exotic forestry or farming project in developing countries. Be extremely cautious with these types of investments. You might receive your first dividend and even the second dividend installment (usually financed by later joining suckers) and then it suddenly stops.

Recall the principles of investing -- regardless of tax and dividend benefits -- never lose money!

Note that dividend payments are the least tax-beneficial way to investing. You will get taxed twice before you might consider reinvesting your returns. There is a good reason why people made fortunes investing and holding to their investments in Apple or Berkshire, which was that they were able to reinvest the returns at much higher compound rates than an average investor could ever achieve.

Consider this: amateur investors usually start investing when they see high dividend yields. The price has dropped and, yet, these companies show up paying high dividend yields. The only point they seem to be forgetting is that the company will most likely stop paying dividends for an undeclared period of time. This is the very reason why the share price dropped dramatically.

Take the case of Volkswagen, who got ravaged by a CO_2 manipulation scandal in September 2015. It was a perfect dividend-paying company with many income investors as shareholders. They lost horrendously in the share price massacre that took place between September and October 2015, only to later see their dividends cut completely. In the end, many income investors ended up with no dividend and enormous share price losses.

It is a dirty little secret that 80/20 Investors are usually buyers of shares sold by income investors. They often buy from disgruntled dividend investors, who just want to close a chapter and get on with their lives. Loss of dividends and declining share prices are just too much for weak dividend income investors.

For any asset, there is a season for buying and a season for selling. Follow the three steps and principles laid down in this book and search for dividend-paying stocks when the time is right. Become a Mr. Womack and not a Mr. Standingback.

What are the remaining 80% tasks?

That will be discussed in my book for advanced investors. I will describe how you could spend the remaining 80% of your investment work, if you find the passion for it and commit the needed time and resources. I will also describe more advanced topics such as single company valuations, single company crises, special situations investments, along with many other ideas in comprehensive case studies and investment anecdotes. This is the territory where you start competing with professionals, and it is only for the advanced, full-time investor, with a passion for research, financial markets, and investing in general.

ACKNOWLEDGMENTS

My most grateful thanks to Mr. Standingback, whose real Identity will be kept secret. Thank you for your honest and inspiring story. I am humbled by your hard work, knack for saving, and willingness to take risks. I hope some of the ideas presented in this work will be as much as of a joy for you to use as they were for me to formulate.

To all my friends and editors, who not only helped me compile and edit this book, but also inspired me to push forward. Special thanks to Subodhana Wijeyeratne, Jeffrey Guthrie, Valerie Smith, Christopher Vitalis and Rene Sakata Schaum - all part of my trusted project team at the thewritingale.com.

I want to express my gratitude to my extended launch team who has made a contribution to the manuscript and book launch, especially Mervyn Teo, Dennis Felgentreff, Markus Ilg, Christopher Baron Moriyama and Aggelos GkOne and many more.

Special thanks to my editing team at craftyourcontent.com, led by Elisa Doucette, and Mike Fishbein for coordinating my launch project.

And to hands down the best community I have ever joined - my trusted supporters in the DC community who all follow a very simple law -- the law of abundance. Special thanks to Brendan Tully, who was willing to spare some time for an interview, and to Taylor Pearson for reading the first manuscript. He is one of the talented new authors I am excited to see become one of the great business authors. Dan Andrews, Michael Smith, Anders Fabech Rønnau, Christopher Gimmer, Karsten Aichholz, John Cavendish, Marco Zamboni, Robert Hopman, Julius Haralampou, Dustin Overback, Tal Gur, Glen Thomson, Paul Levine, Mervyn Teo, Kate Hill, Jeremy Ginsburg, Dave Furness and many more.

Special thanks goes to Tatsuro Tsushima, my Japanese innovation mentor, who helped me simplify many concepts and inspired me to look deeper into the principles of innovation, the concept of disruptive innovation and ethical entrepreneurship.

I am in debt to Michael Brodie-Brown and Nick Heidfeld, who showed patience, understanding, and financed my education. Without them, this book would have never happened.

My family, especially my mother, who like any mother has deep protective instincts for her children, but has to deal with a son who went out to see the world, and too often neglects his family.

BIBLIOGRAPHY

1. Hogan, M, How Mr. Womack Made a Killing (1978) *Forbes Magazine*. The story of Mr. Womack, "How Mr. Womack Made a Killing" was reprinted by *Forbes Magazine* in October, 1978. It was originally a letter sent to John Train, a famous investment author, by Melvid Hogan himself. It is a wonderful story that illustrates an investment philosophy now long forgotten.

2. Koch, R. *Living the 80/20 way, new edition: work less, worry less, succeed More, enjoy more.* (2004). Yarmouth, UK: Nicholas Brealey Publishing, p. 98.

3. Annualized Return: 'Annualized Total Return' The average amount of money earned by an investment each year over a given time period. Calculated as Compound Annual Growth Rate (CAGR). This is the mean annual growth rate of an investment over a specified period of time longer than one year.

4. Koch, R. *Living the 80/20 way, new edition: work less, worry less, succeed More, enjoy more.* (2004). Yarmouth, UK: Nicholas Brealey Publishing, p. 96.

5. Marshall, P. (2013). *80/20 Sales and marketing: the definitive guide to working less and making more.* US: Entrepreneur Press, p 4.

6. Koch, R. *Living the 80/20 way, new edition: work less, worry less, succeed More, enjoy more.* (2004). Yarmouth, UK: Nicholas Brealey Publishing, p. 52.

7. Ellis, C.D. *The elements of investing – easy lessons for every investor.* (2010). Hobocken, NJ: John Wiley & Sons, Inc.

8. International Monetary Fund. (2012, October) *World Economic Outlook Database.* Retrieved from IMF website https://www.imf.org.

9. Byanyima, W, "62 people own the same as half the world, reveals Oxfam Davos report", published January 18, 2016, oxfam.org

10. Russell, R. Rich man poor man. *Dow Theory Letters.* Retrieved from http://dowtheoryletters.com/Content_Free/2494.aspx

11. Malkiel, B.G. (2007). *Random walk down wall street: the time tested strategy for successful investing.* New York, NY: W.W. Norton & Company, Inc.

12. Graham, B. (2006). *The intelligent investor: the definitive book on value investing.* New York, NY: HarperCollins Publishing, Inc., p. 79.

13. Markowitz, H, Portfolio Selection, The Journal of Finance, Vol. 7, No. 1. (Mar., 1952), pp. 77-91.

14. Hammurabi. (1754 BC). The code of hammurabi. *The Avalon Project: Documents in Law, History and Diplomacy*. Retrieved from http://avalon.law.yale.edu/ancient/hamframe.asp

15. Plutarch. (1916). *Plutarch, lives: Pericles and Fabius Maximus, Nicias and Crassus*. Cambridge, MA: Harvard University Press, p. 317.

16. Baladouni, V. (1983). Accounting in the early years of the East India Company. *The Accounting Historians Journal*, 10.2, 63–80. Retrieved from http://www.jstor.org/stable/40697780

17. Wilson, D.A. (1988). *Rothschild: the wealth and power of a dynasty*. New York, NY: Scribner, p. 24.

18. Rogers, J.(2003). *Adventure capitalist: the ultimate road trip*. New York, NY: Random House.

19. Wilson, D.A. (1988). *Rothschild: the wealth and power of a dynasty*. New York, NY: Scribner, p. 200.

20. Rosenblum, C. (2004). 'Hetty': Scrooge in Hoboken. *The New York Times*. Retrieved from http://www.nytimes.com/2004/12/19/books/review/hetty-scrooge-in-hoboken.html

Hetty Green was a rarity--a woman who largely through her own efforts amassed a ton of money during the Gilded Age, a time when virtually everyone else getting rich -- Rockefeller, Morgan, Carnegie -- was a man.

21. Leavitt, J.A. (1985). *American women managers and administrators: a selective biographical dictionary of twentieth-century leaders in business, education, and government*. Westport, CT: Greenwood Publishing Group, p. 93.

22. Phalon, R. (2001). *Greatest investing stories*. New York, NY: John Wiley & Sons, Inc. p.146.

23. Phalon, R. (2001). *Greatest investing stories*. New York, NY: John Wiley & Sons, Inc. p.146.

24. Phalon, R. (2001). *Greatest investing stories*. New York, NY: John Wiley & Sons, Inc. p.146.

25. Getty, J. P. (1965). *How to be rich*. US: Playboy Press.

26. Getty, J. P. (1965). *How to be rich*. US: Playboy Press.

27. NYO staff. (2003). The brain behind teledyne, a great American capitalist - *Grant's Interest Rate Observer*. Retrieved from

http://observer.com/2003/04/the-brain-behind-teledyne-a-great-american-capitalist/

28. Buffet, W. (1984, Fall) The superinvestors of Graham-and-Doddsville. *Hermes: the Columbia Business School Magazine*, 4-15.

29. Kilpatrick, A. (2007). *Of permanent value: the story of Warren Buffett*. Birmingham, AL: Andrew Kilpatrick, p. 93.
In 1962, the Buffett Partnership began buying Berkshire Hathaway at under $8 a share.

30. He continued as CEO and Chairman of Berkshire Hathaway and kept some of his core position in Berkshires Names and for his private portfolio, which declined during the recession. Furthermore, his Berkshire shares declined more than general market averages during the same period.

31. Forbes Staff (2008). Warren Buffett--In 1974. Retrieved from http://www.forbes.com/2008/04/30/warren-buffett-profile-invest-oped-cx_hs_0430buffett.html

32. Smith, A. (1972). *Supermoney*. Hoboken, NJ: John Wiley & Sons, Inc.

33. SEC, Questions Advisers Should Ask While Establishing or Reviewing Their Compliance Programs (2006). Retrieved from https://www.sec.gov/info/cco/adviser_compliance_questions.htm

34. Bogle, J. [Presentation]. (2013). *Address to the Boston Security Analysts Society*.

35. Xie, Y. (2015). Goldman's BRIC era ends as fund folds after years of losses. *Bloomberg*. Retreived from http://www.bloomberg.com/news/articles/2015-11-08/goldman-s-bric-era-ends-as-fund-closes-after-years-of-losses

36. Syer, S. (2014). Fidelity's Will Danoff: the $110 billion manager. *The Boston Globe*. Retrieved from https://www.bostonglobe.com/business/2014/11/11/fidelity-will-danoff-billion-man/SJEP7CuMKcw4bjkJdiwNMP/story.html

37. Johnson Associates Inc, Survey among clients conducted in 2013. Retrieved from http://www.bloomberg.com/news/articles/2013-10-28/goldman-sachs-encourages-junior-bankers-to-take-weekends-off
Analysts typically make base salaries in a range of $70,000 to $90,000, with bonuses bringing the total compensation figure to as much as $140,000, according to New York-based compensation consultant Johnson Associates Inc.

38. Schneider, David. Interview with an industry professional working on the sell side. Hong Kong, 2015.

39. Mitchel, C. (2015). What's the day trading success rate? the thorough answer. *Vantage Point Trading*. Retrieved from http://vantagepointtrading.com/archives/13922

40. Keynes, J.M. (1936). *The general theory of employment, interest and money*. London, UK: Palgrave Macmillan.

41. Page, S. (2015). Ben Bernanke: more execs should have gone to jail for causing Great Recession. *USA Today*. Retrieved from http://www.usatoday.com/story/news/politics/2015/10/04/ben-bernanke-execs-jail-great-recession-federal-reserve/72959402/

42. Stanley, T.J. (1998), The Millionaire Next Door. US: Gallery Books

43. Clason, G.S. (1926). *The richest man in babylon*. London, UK: Thinking Ink Limited.

44. In Singapore, the Central Provident Fund (CPF) is a compulsory comprehensive savings plan for working Singaporeans and permanent residents primarily to fund their retirement, healthcare, and housing needs.

45. 2009 pabrai funds annual meeting transcript - Buffett introduced Pabrai to Munger. (2011). *Guru Focus*. Retrieved from http://www.gurufocus.com/news/119367/2009-pabrai-funds-annual-meeting-transcript--buffett-introduced-pabrai-to-munger

46. Charlie Munger and Warren Buffett at the 1996 Annual Meeting of Berkshire Hathaway

47. Chambers, D, & Elroy, D. (2013). Retrospectives: John Maynard Keynes, Investment Innovator. *Journal of Economic Perspectives*, 27.3, 213-28.

48. Gladwell, M, (2011) Outliers: The Story of Success, New York: Back Bay Books

49. Rubin, R.E. (2003) In an Uncertain World: Tough Choices from Wall Street to Washington, New York: Random House; First Edition edition

50. Lowe, J. (2003). *Damn right!: behind the scenes with berkshire hathaway billionaire Charlie Munger*. New York, NY: John Wiley & Sons, Inc., p. 153.

51. Olson, P. (2014). Finding Alibaba: how Jerry Yang made the most lucrative bet in Silicon Valley history. *Forbes*. Retrieved from http://www.forbes.com/sites/parmyolson/2014/09/30/how-jerry-yang-

made-the-most-lucrative-bet-in-tech-
history/#2715e4857a0b14e711513aed

52. Olson, P. (2014). Finding Alibaba: how Jerry Yang made the most lucrative bet in Silicon Valley history. *Forbes*. Retrieved from http://www.forbes.com/sites/parmyolson/2014/09/30/how-jerry-yang-made-the-most-lucrative-bet-in-tech-history/#2715e4857a0b14e711513aed

53. Helft, Miguel. (2014). Jerry Yang: the most successful American investor in China? *Fortune*. Retrieved from http://fortune.com/2014/09/18/jerry-yang-the-most-successful-american-investor-in-china/

54. Novellino, T. (2014). Inside Jerry Yang's wild bet on Alibaba and Jack Ma. *Upstart Business Journal*. Retrieved from http://upstart.bizjournals.com/entrepreneurs/hot-shots/2014/10/01/inside-jerry-yang-s-wild-bet-on-alibaba-jack-ma.html?page=all.

55. Schneider, David. Interview with Brendan Tully of The Search Engine Shop. December, 2015.

56. Lewis, M. (1989) Liar's Poker: Rising Through the Wreckage on Wall Street, New York: W. W. Norton & Company

57. Lancher, D, Secrets of Sovereign, Institutional Investor – March 2006 International Edition

58. Business Section. International Herald Tribune – March 13, 2003 .

59. Wittriech J. A. (1987) Often attributed to Mark Twain, but the earliest published source yet located is by Joseph Anthony Wittreich in Feminist Milton (1987)

60. Quinn, J. (2009). Profile: Carlos Slim. *Telegraph*. Retrieved from http://www.telegraph.co.uk/news/newstopics/profiles/4317646/Profile-Carlos-Slim.html

61. Lowenstein, R. (1995). *Buffett: the making of an american capitalist*. New York, NY: Random House.

62. Rothchild, J. (1996). When the shoeshine boys talk stocks it was a great sell signal in 1929. So what are the shoeshine boys talking about now? *Fortune*. Retrieved from http://archive.fortune.com/magazines/fortune/fortune_archive/1996/04/15/211503/index.htm

63. Baruch, B.M. (1957). *Baruch: my own story*. New York, NY: Henry Holt and Company.

64. El Issa, E. (2015). American household credit card debt statistics: 2015. *Nerdwallet*. Retrieved from http://www.nerdwallet.com/blog/credit-card-data/average-credit-card-debt-household/

65. Getty, J. P. (1965). *How to be rich*. US: Playboy Press.

66. Lynch, P. (2000). One up on Wall Street: how To use what you already know to make money in the market. New York, NY: Simon & Schuster.

67. Aeschylus. (458 BC) *The Oresteia*. Aeschylus (525 BC – 456 BC) was a playwright of ancient Greece. In his play *The Oresteia,* Agamemnon states: "Zeus, who guided mortals to be wise, has established his fixed law— wisdom comes through suffering."

68. Cialdini, R. B. (2006) Influence: The Psychology of Persuasion, Revised Edition Revised Edition, New York: Harper Business

69. Markowitz, H, Portfolio Selection, The Journal of Finance, Vol. 7, No. 1. (Mar., 1952), pp. 77-91.

ABOUT THE AUTHOR

David Schneider trained as banker in Germany and has studied financial services in London and Tokyo. He worked in investment banking and asset management for fifteen years and co-founded two hedge funds. Since 2011 he has become an independent investor and a location-independent entrepreneur and writer. His mission is simple: to use the 80/20 principle to educate people on how to handle their own financial affairs in the fields of saving, investing, and risk management.

He is the founder of nomdaicinvestor.com and senior contributor at honestnomads.com, traveling the world to find and research business trends and investment opportunities on the ground.

CONTACT THE AUTHOR:

Facebook
https://www.facebook.com/NomadicInvestor/

Twitter
https://twitter.com/WooSchneider

LinkedIn
https://jp.linkedin.com/in/WooSchneider

Made in the USA
San Bernardino, CA
27 June 2016